THE USBORNE CHILDREN'S ENCYCLOPEDIA

Jane Elliott and Colin King

With the help of Susan Crawford and Annabel Craig

Research by Ingrid Cranfield

Designed by Sylvia Tate

Edited by Angela Wilkes

Contents

What is the Earth?

The Earth is a huge ball of rock spinning in space. It is not a perfect ball as it is flattened at the top and bottom. The equator is an imaginary line around the widest part of the Earth. The top half of the Earth is called the northern hemisphere and the bottom half is called the southern hemisphere.

Earth Facts

The Earth measures about 40,000 km around the equator. It would take a month to drive around it at 55 km per hour.

The Earth weighs about 6,000 million, million million tonnes.

The highest temperature ever recorded was 57.7°C in the Sahara Desert. This is hot enough to fry an egg on the sand.

The lowest temperature ever recorded was minus 88.3°C in Antarctica.

One fifth of the land is desert. Deserts are the hottest and driest places on Earth. They have less than 25 cm rain a year.

Near the equator it is hot all the year round and it rains nearly every day. The land around the equator is called the Tropics.

Thick, green forests called rainforests grow in the Tropics. Tropical rainforests contain over half of all the types of plants and animals in the world.

Only about a quarter of the Earth's surface is land. There are seven big pieces of land, called continents. Most of the land is in the northern hemisphere.

Nearly three-quarters of the Earth's surface is covered by sea. The four oceans are all joined together. You could sail right round the Earth without seeing land.

Many mountains are too high and cold for plants and animals to survive there. Mount Everest, the highest mountain on Earth, is 8,848 metres high.

About a tenth of the Earth's surface is always covered with ice. The further you travel from the equator, the colder it is. The Poles are the coldest places on Earth.

Air and the atmosphere

The Earth is surrounded by a layer of air about 500 kilometres thick, called the atmosphere. It stops dangerous rays from the Sun from burning up life on Earth.

We cannot see air but we feel it as wind. It is made up of many gases, such as oxygen, which we breathe, and carbon dioxide, which is used by plants.

The higher you go into the atmosphere, the less air there is and the harder it is to breathe. That is why people carry oxygen tanks when they climb mountains.

All our weather happens in the ten kilometres of the atmosphere closest to the Earth. Planes usually fly higher than the weather, 13-22 kilometres above the Earth.

The Earth in Space

The Solar System

The Earth is one of nine planets that circle the Sun. They are kept in orbit by the pull of the Sun's gravity*.

Together they make up the Solar System. It was probably formed from dust and gases billions of years ago.

Mars is sometimes called the Red Planet because it is made of red rocks.

Earth is probably the only planet which has water.

Mercury is the planet closest to the Sun. It is a bit bigger than our moon.

Venus is so bright it is often mistaken for a UFO (unidentified flying object.) Its surface is hidden by thick, white clouds.

Jupiter and Saturn are made of gases and liquids and do not have hard surfaces.

What does the Sun do?

The Sun gives the Earth light and warmth. Without it the Earth would be in constant darkness and too icy cold for anything to survive.

The Sun is so far away that it takes eight minutes for its rays to reach Earth. It is so big that you could fit over a million Earths into it.

How hot is the Sun?

The Sun is a gigantic ball of burning gases. Its surface temperature is 6000°C. A pin head as hot as this could kill you from 150 km away.

The asteroids are thousands of rocks which go round the Sun between Mars and Jupiter.

Plan it!

Use this chart to work out the order of the planets from biggest to smallest. Which one takes the longest to orbit the Sun? Which one is the furthest away from the Sun?

Name of planet	Diameter	Distance from the sun	How long to orbit the Sun
	kilometres	kilometres	years
Pluto	3,000*	5950 million	248 years
Neptune	48,400	4497 million	165 years
Uranus	52,000	2870 million	84 years
Saturn	120,860	1427 million	29.5 years
Jupiter	142,800	778 million	12 years
Mars	6,790	228 million	687 days
Earth	12,756	150 million	365 days
Venus	12,100	108 million	225 days
Mercury	4,880	58 million	88 days

Neptune and Uranus are made of gases. They are so far from the sun that they are dark and frozen places.

Uranus is circled by nine rings.

Pluto was the last planet to be discovered. It was first sighted in 1930.

Saturn is circled by huge rings made of pieces of rock and ice. It has ten moons, one of which is nearly as big as Mercury.

Sunspots and solar flares

Sunspots are made by areas of gas which are cooler than the rest of the Sun's surface. Solar flares are giant jets of gas that shoot up millions of miles.

WARNING Never look directly at the Sun as its brightness could damage your eyes.

Watching an eclipse

SUN   MOON   EARTH

If you watched the sky for about 360 years from the same place, you would see a complete eclipse of the Sun. This is when the new moon moves directly in front of the Sun and blocks off its light from the Sun.

*Approximate measurement

5

Moons

A moon is a ball of rock that circles a planet. Most of the planets in our solar system have moons. You can see them on pages 4-5.

Our moon does not shine with a light of its own but is lit up by light from the Sun.

The dark side of the moon

We never see one side of the moon, because the same side is always facing the Earth.

The moon's far side was a mystery until photographed by satellite in the 1960s.

Does the moon change shape?

The Sun lights up different parts of the moon as it orbits the Earth. The moon does not really change shape at all.

It takes the moon 27.3 days to circle the Earth. The different 'shapes' of the moon are called phases.

When the Sun shines on the far side of the moon, you can hardly see the moon in the sky. This is called a new moon.

Each night for the next two weeks more and more of the moon is lit up as it travels around the Earth.

When the moon is halfway around the Earth, its whole face is lit up. Now it is called a full moon.

Over the next two weeks, the moon shrinks in the sky as less and less of it is lit up. Soon it will begin its orbit again.

Who is the man in the moon?

It looks as if the moon has a face because rocks make shadows on the surface.

Eclipse of the moon

SUN EARTH MOON

An eclipse of the moon only happens when the moon is full and moves into the Earth's shadow.

Because the Sun's light cannot reach it, the moon looks as if it has vanished.

Stars

A star is born

Scientists think that a star begins its life as space dust which forms a ball and turns to gas. The gas burns, which makes the star shine. It may shine for 10,000 million years.

As the gas is used up, the star swells to 50 times its normal size. Finally it explodes, or cools down and shrinks. The tiny star, now called a white dwarf, is almost dead.

Measuring the Milky Way

OUR SOLAR SYSTEM IS SOMEWHERE HERE

Our sun is a star in a galaxy (star family) called the Milky Way. The Milky Way has 100,000 million stars. Scientists think there may be more than 6,000 million galaxies.

Huge distances in space are measured in light years. Light travels nine million, million km a year. This craft from another galaxy, flying as fast as light, will reach us in a million years.

How do we know?

Astronomers are scientists who study the stars. Until recently they only had their eyes and simple telescopes to rely upon.

Now satellites orbit in space. They send information about our weather and relay messages around the world. Space probes are sent to explore the planets.

Manned space shuttles take off like rockets and land like gliders. They carry all sorts of useful scientific equipment into space.

Comets and Meteors

Comets sometimes appear as they orbit the Sun. They are made of ice and rock and have long tails.

A shooting star is a meteor or rock burning as it enters the Earth's atmosphere. Meteors were once part of a comet.

How the land moves

How old is the Earth?

The Earth was formed about 4,600 million years ago. At first it was a fiery mixture of boiling rock and poisonous gases.

As millions of years went by, the Earth grew cooler and a thin crust formed on its surface, which sealed in the heat.

What is inside the Earth?

IT IS 6,300 KM (3,900M) TO THE CENTRE OF THE EARTH. THE TEMPERATURE THERE IS AS HOT AS THE SUN.

THE EARTH'S INNER CORE IS A SOLID BALL OF IRON. THE OUTER CORE IS MADE UP OF HOT LIQUID METALS.

THE MANTLE IS A LAYER OF SOFT FLOWING ROCK. IT IS HOT AND LIQUID TOWARDS THE TOP.

THE CRUST IS MADE OF HARD ROCK WHICH IS SPLIT INTO SECTIONS CALLED PLATES. THEY CARRY THE LAND AND THE OCEANS.

How Mountains are made

Mountains take millions of years to form. Sometimes the Earth's crust is squeezed and forms fold mountains.

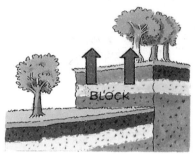

BLOCK

Block mountains form when the Earth's crust splits and one side is pushed up.

DOME

Dome mountains form when melted rock below the Earth's crust slowly forces land upwards.

Whatever happened to supercontinent?

Scientists think the continents may once have been joined together as a continent called Pangaea.

About 190 million years ago movements in the Earth's crust made it break up. Pieces of it are still moving apart.

AMERICA

AFRICA

Earthquakes and volcanoes

When the ground trembles and shakes it is called an earthquake. Earthquakes can split and crack the ground, destroy buildings and cause floods and fires.

A volcano is a place where red hot, liquid rock, called lava, ashes and gases force their way up a crack from deep inside the Earth. The lava hardens as it cools, to form a mountain.

GEYSERS AND MUDSPRINGS ARE FOUND NEAR VOLCANOES. STEAM AND BOILING MUD ARE SIGNS OF THE EARTH'S HEAT ESCAPING.

80 OF THE 850 ACTIVE VOLCANOES ARE UNDER THE SEA. SCIENTISTS TRY TO PREDICT WHEN THE SLEEPING (DORMANT) ONES WILL ERUPT AGAIN.

Earthquakes and volcanoes often occur close together along fault lines in the Earth's crust (see the diagram on the opposite page).

A fault line is where two plates of the Earth's crust rub against each other deep down and make the ground move.

Whizzers

The volcano Paricutin suddenly erupted in Mexico in 1943. Within two years it grew 457 metres high and 16 kilometres wide. Every day it blew out 100,000 tons of lava.

Bangers

After sleeping for 200 years, Krakatoa in Indonesia exploded in 1883. The explosion caused a tidal wave 41 metres high which killed over 36,000 people.

9

Under the ground

Burrowing down

The Earth's crust has several layers. The top layer is soil, which is made of crushed rock and the remains of plants.

SMALL ANIMALS, PLANTS AND INSECTS BURROW INTO THE SOIL, AND HELP TO BREAK IT UP.

BELOW THE SOIL THERE IS A SMALL LAYER OF STONES.

UNDERNEATH EVERYTHING THERE IS A LAYER OF SOLID ROCK.

How are rocks made?

A rock is a mixture of different minerals. Different rocks are formed in different ways. There are three main types of rock – igneous, metamorphic and sedimentary ones.

Igneous rock

Hot, molten rocks from deep inside the Earth are thrown out by volcanoes, then cool and harden into rock.

Sedimentary rock

Rock that has built up in layers. It is made from bits of rock, sand or shells which have been washed into the sea or a lake.

Metamorphic rock

Rocks that have changed in some way after being heated or squeezed deep inside the Earth.

These bits of rock sink to the bottom and over millions of years they harden together into solid rock.

Earthquakes sometimes force sedimentary rock up from the sea-bed so it becomes part of the land.

Mineral crystals

Some minerals do not form rocks. They grow into mineral crystals under the ground. Each mineral has different shaped crystals.

Everyday minerals

These minerals are used daily all over the world.

Precious minerals

Gemstones are very hard and beautiful. They are worth a lot of money.

Wearing down the land

Frost, ice, wind and rain all slowly break rocks down into smaller pieces. This wearing down of the Earth's surface is called erosion.

OLD, WEATHER-BEATEN MOUNTAINS ARE USUALLY LOWER AND MORE ROUNDED THAN RECENTLY FORMED ONES.

CAVES ARE FORMED BY WATER WEARING AWAY ROCK UNDER THE GROUND.

THE WEATHER OFTEN WEARS ROCKS INTO STRANGE SHAPES.

Why do we mine?

People mine minerals because they are both useful and worth a lot of money.

Oil and natural gas have been formed over millions of years from tiny sea animals which were preserved in rock.

Metal minerals, such as gold and silver, have to be separated from rock before they can be used.

Coal is the remnants of ancient swamp plants that were preserved in rock and hardened over millions of years.

Finding fossils

Fossils are the remains of plants and animals which were preserved in rock. They are millions of years old.

Scientists study fossils to find out how the Earth has changed and about plants and animals which lived on it.

Both the soft and hard parts of a creature can be preserved, but sometimes all that is left is a print of its shape or feet.

Time

Why do we have day and night?

The Sun's light gives the Earth its day and night. The Earth spins like a top in space at 960 kph. It takes 24 hours to spin around once.

AS IT SPINS, IT IS NIGHT ON THE SIDE OF THE EARTH THAT FACES AWAY FROM THE SUN.

MOON

IT IS DAY ON THE SIDE OF THE EARTH THAT FACES THE SUN.

Where do the stars go?

During the day the stars are still in the sky but we cannot see them because the Sun's light is much brighter than they are.

Why does the Sun set?

The Sun does not really move at all. Because the Earth spins, it looks as if the Sun rises in the east and sets in the west.

Me and my shadow

Light always shines in straight lines, so you see dark shadows behind anything which stands in its way.

MORNING

AT MIDDAY THE SUN IS DIRECTLY OVERHEAD AND THE SHADOWS ARE VERY SHORT

MIDDAY

EARLY IN THE MORNING AND EVENING THE SUN IS LOW IN THE SKY, SO THE SHADOWS ARE LONG.

EVENING

Ways of measuring time

Long ago hunters kept track of how long they were away by counting how many times they went to sleep at night.

Knights used a sand timer to time a tournament. It ended when the sand had run from the top half to the bottom.

People used sundials. During the day the Sun's shadow is cast on to the dial and moves around to mark the time.

Going clock wise

The Egyptians divided day and night into hours. They measured a stick's shadow against an hour scale.

At night they filled a pot with water. As the water ran out through a tiny hole they read the hour marks on the side.

It was hard for people to meet when they all measured time differently. They needed a standard measure of time.

In 1581 Galileo, an Italian, watched a lamp swing. He noticed that its swing always took the same time, no matter how big it was.

So the pendulum clock was invented, which can measure time accurately, by the swinging pendulum. People have used clocks ever since.

Nowadays clocks are even more accurate and scientists can build atomic clocks that only lose one second in 1,700,000 years.

Keeping up with the times

Every minute of the day somewhere around the world there is a sunrise, a sunset, a midday or a midnight.

When flying east, you put your watch forward an hour each time you cross a zone. When flying west you put your watch back an hour.

The world is divided into 24 time zones. Lines of longitude divide the zones on a map. The gaps between them show how far the Earth spins in one hour.

If you cross the International Dateline you change your calendar, not your watch. You lose a day going west and gain a day going east.

13

Why do the seasons change?

The Earth always tilts to one side as it spins around the Sun and this gives us the different seasons.

It is summer in the hemisphere that is tilted towards the Sun and winter in the other one.

Autumn and spring are the in-between seasons when the two hemispheres are the same distance from the Sun.

Sandman or snowman?

The two hemispheres always have opposite seasons from each other. When it is summer in one, it is winter in the other.

Long days and short days

Summer days are longer than winter ones because the hemisphere tilting towards the Sun stays in the Sun's light for longer.

The land of the midnight sun

Because of the Earth's tilt, the Sun's rays are always spread out at the Poles, so it is always cold and icy there.

It is dark for nearly 24 hours a day in the winter. In the summer the Sun shines all night as well as all day.

About 300 years ago some British criminals begged to be hanged rather than sent to spend the winter in the dark.

It never rains but it pours

The Equator is never tilted away from the Sun. The Sun's rays shine directly on to it, so it is always hot there.

Places close to the Equator do not have a summer and winter. They just have a dry season and a rainy season.

In the rainy season, winds blow in from the sea, bringing moisture. They blow the other way in the dry season.

Seasonal changes

Winter

Winter is the coldest season. The days are short and it gets dark very early. There is snow and frost in many countries.

Plants stop growing and the trees are bare of leaves. Some animals grow thick coats to help them keep warm.

Other animals sleep all winter. People wear warm clothes and spend most of their time indoors.

Spring

The days grow longer and warmer. Buds appear on the trees, bulbs flower and plants begin to grow again.

Birds that have spent the winter in warmer countries return, build their nests and lay their eggs.

Animals look for mates and have their babies. People do more things outside again in the warmer weather.

Summer

Summer is the warmest time of year. The days are long and it does not get dark until late. Everything grows well.

Flowers bloom, fruit ripens on the trees and crops ripen in the fields. There is plenty for birds and animals to eat.

People spend more time outside enjoying the sunshine. Many of them go on holiday to places such as the seaside.

Autumn

The days begin to get shorter and colder. Plants stop flowering and leaves begin to fall from the trees.

There is plenty of fruit and berries on the trees and bushes. The crops are harvested and the fields are ploughed.

Many animals and farmers store food for the winter months. Some birds fly away to warmer countries.

Weather

What is weather?

Our daily weather is caused by a mixture of three things: Sun, air and water. The Sun gives us warmth, the air moves to make the wind and water makes the clouds, rain and snow.

The same rain over again

The rain you see has fallen millions of times before. Follow the water on its journey to see how the Earth uses the same water over and over again.

The Sun

Every day the Sun heats up millions of gallons of water from the sea and rivers. This makes tiny, invisible drops of moisture rise up into the air.

Clouds

As the warm air rises, it cools down. The tiny drops of moisture turn into millions of larger drops of water which join together to form clouds.

Cloud clues

Cumulus mean fine weather. They are white and fluffy. Large, dark ones usually bring bad weather.

Stratus is usually a layer of thin, pale grey cloud covering the whole sky. It is often a sign of light rain or drizzle.

Nimbus are grey rain clouds with ragged edges. Some have white tops like cauliflower heads and may mean storms.

Hurricanes and tornadoes

A giant tropical storm, a hurricane, is a great whirling mass of air which can uproot trees and destroy buildings.

A tornado, or whirlwind, is smaller, but faster and just as dangerous. It will suck up or destroy anything in its path.

Waterspouts are tornadoes over water, often very tall. People have mistaken them for sea monsters.

Hailstones are frozen raindrops. They blow about in the clouds and build up layers of ice round them before they fall.

Fog and mist are clouds close to the ground.

Rain

As the air becomes colder, more drops of water form. When there are enough, they become too heavy for the cloud and fall to the ground as rain.

Snow

Snowflakes and raindrops are made the same way but when it is very cold, the water drops freeze to form ice crystals and fall from the clouds as snow.

The rain and melted snow flow into streams and rivers and are carried back to the lakes and oceans. Then the water begins its journey all over again.

Cirrus are usually wispy and streaky. They are a sign of wind. They float very high up and are made of ice crystals.

Why the wind blows

When air is warm, it rises and cold air flows in beneath it. When air moves around like this it makes wind.

Some winds blow right across the world as hot air from the Equator rises and is replaced by cold air from the Poles.

Thunder and lightning

When the weather is bad, electricity builds up inside a cloud. Lightning is a giant spark of electricity escaping.

The lightning heats the air around it. The hot air pushes against the cooler air and makes the sound of thunder.

Rainbows*

You see a rainbow when the sun shines through raindrops. The colours are always in the same order: red, orange, yellow, green, blue, indigo and violet.

*You can find out more about rainbows on page 104/5.

Climate

Why are there hot and cold places?

Weather is how much rain or sunshine a place has every day. When people talk about climate, they mean the usual type of weather a place has.

How hot or cold a place is depends on how far it is from the Equator*, where it is always hot, but other things can also affect the climate.

Land far from sea is often dry, as sea winds do not carry their moisture that far. In the middle of a continent the summers are hot and the winters cold.

Land near the sea has cooler summers and warmer winters than inland. The climate can be affected by warm or cold ocean currents flowing near the coast.

It usually rains a lot near mountains and the higher you go, the colder it becomes. High mountains on the Equator have snowy peaks all the year round.

Steamy rainforests

Rainforests (or jungles) grow in the Tropics near the Equator, where it is very hot and rains heavily every day.

Plants and trees grow fast and very close together there. Plants can grow to the size of trees and the trees are amongst the tallest in the world.

The forests teem with all sorts of plants and creatures that do not live anywhere else in the world. Many of them are in danger of dying out.

Few people live in rainforests as it is too hot and sticky there. Tribes have to live on plants they find, and hunt whichever animals they can.

*You can find out more about the Equator on page 2.

Life in the deserts

Most deserts are in the Tropics. They are the hottest and driest places on Earth and very few things can survive there.

CAMELS CAN SURVIVE FOR DAYS WITHOUT WATER. THEY LIVE ON FOOD OR FAT STORED IN THEIR HUMPS.

There are two types of desert — rocky deserts and sandy deserts. Sandy deserts are not always flat as the wind blows the sand into hills called dunes.

It rains very rarely and when it does there are usually violent thunderstorms and floods. One desert in Peru had no rain for 400 years.

An oasis is a waterhole where people take their animals to drink. Farmers grow crops and date trees there. Oases often become towns.

The Poles

The North and South Poles are the coldest places on Earth. There is frozen land at the South Pole, but at the North Pole there is just a huge slab of ice floating in the Arctic Ocean.

Icebergs often break away from the sheets of ice and float away until they melt. More than three-quarters of an iceberg are hidden below the water.

Eskimoes live near the North Pole. The only land animals at the South Pole are visiting scientists, but penguins, whales and seals live in the seas.

If the ice at the Poles melted, the seas would rise by over 33 metres. This would be enough to completely submerge New York, London and Paris.

Rivers and lakes

Rowing down the river

Every river starts off as a spring flowing out of a hillside or as a stream from a lake.

As the stream flows downhill, rainwater and other streams flow into it, making it swell.

At the beginning of its journey the young river flows through narrow valleys with steep sides.

It carries rocks and sand with it and these grind away the banks on each side.

As the river grows larger, it wears away more land and the valleys become wider.

Most rivers wind their way downhill to the sea, usually along the easiest courses.

At the sea

Some rivers fork out near the sea. This type of river mouth is called a delta.

The place where the river flows into the sea is called the river mouth.

A river mouth where the coastal tides flow in and out twice a day is called an estuary.

Lakes

A lake is a hollow filled with water. Sometimes it is water that was left behind when a river changed its course.

Lake Baykal in Central Siberia, USSR, is the deepest lake in the world. It is 1,940 metres deep at its deepest part.

New Zealanders used to swim in the crater lake of an active volcano. The volcano kept the water hot.

Floods

Rivers can flood and cause damage. The Hwang Ho river in China once flooded and changed its course by 480 km.

A flood barrier has been built across the River Thames in England, to stop very high tides from flooding London.

Some rivers are blocked by dams, which make hydro-electric power. Lakes form behind the dams.

Frozen rivers

A glacier is a river of ice that moves very slowly down a mountain in winter and melts back a little in summer.

Most glaciers only move a few centimetres a day but the Quarayaq Glacier in Greenland moves 20-24 metres a day.

In the Ice Age glaciers moved across the land, carving out valleys and mountains such as the Matterhorn in Switzerland.

Daredevils and waterfalls

When water flows from hard rock on to soft rock, it wears away the soft rock and makes a waterfall, a step in the river.

In 1859 Charles Blondin, a French acrobat, crossed the Niagara Falls on a tightrope 48.8 metres above the water.

In 1929 Al Faussett, an American, went over the 70 metre Shoshone Falls in his canoe and lived to tell the tale.

River records

The longest river in the world is the River Nile in Africa. It is 6,670 km long and flows into the Mediterranean.

The River Amazon is the biggest river in the world. Over 15,000 smaller rivers flow into it on its way to the sea.

The highest waterfall is the Angel Falls in Venezuela. It is 979 metres tall, higher than a 220 storey building.

The Seas

Warm and cold water

The seas cover three-quarters of the Earth's surface. There are warm seas near the Equator and frozen seas in the Arctic. Ocean currents can help to make seas warmer or colder.

Currents are rivers of water that flow in the sea. They drift from hot to cool regions around the world in huge circles. Currents are also caused by the winds and the spin of the Earth.

Why is the sea salty?

Rivers and rainwater wash salty minerals from the land to the sea. Some salts are used by animals to build their shells.

The saltiest seas are small, inland seas. The Dead Sea in Israel is so salty that fish cannot live in it.

If all the seas dried up there would be enough salt left to build a wall round the Equator 282 km high and 1.5 km thick.

What are waves?

Waves are ripples made by the wind. The water seems to move forward but really moves up and down like the sailors' rope.

Waves can travel hundreds of kilometres. They only grow tall and topple over when they come up against land.

Tidal waves are giant waves, up to 10 m high, caused by earthquakes or volcanic explosions underwater.

Tides

On most seashores the height of the water rises and falls twice a day. These changes are called high and low tides and they are caused by the pull of the moon and Sun.

The moon circles the Earth and has a pulling effect on the seas. They rise higher on the side where the moon is, bringing high tides. The other side of the Earth will have low tides.

Underwater lands

If all the water was drained from the sea the sea-bed would look like the land with plains, valleys and mountains.

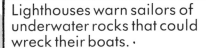

Lighthouses warn sailors of underwater rocks that could wreck their boats.

Coral reefs are walls made from the hard cases of small jelly-like animals called corals. They are found in shallow tropical waters.

An island is really the tip of an underwater mountain sticking up out of the sea.

The highest mountain in the world is the underwater mountain Mauna Kea in Hawaii. It is 10 km high.

The depths of the oceans have hardly been explored at all. They are pitch dark, as no sunlight reaches them.

At Challenger Deep in the Pacific Ocean you would have to wait over an hour for your line to sink 11 km to the ocean floor.

Better late than never

A message in a bottle was thrown overboard off Australia and found 72 years later on a nearby island.

After his ship *Benlomond* sank, Poon Lim, a Chinese seaman, survived on a raft for 133 days before he was rescued.

In 1982 a Tudor fighting ship, the Mary Rose, was salvaged from 12 metres of mud, 400 years after sinking.

You can find out more about life in the seas on page 44.

Explorers

Old ideas about the Earth

The Ancient Eygptians thought the land was a god lying down who had trees and plants sprouting from his body.

They believed that the sky was a huge goddess leaning over him and that the stars were the jewels in her robe.

The Ancient Greeks thought the Earth was a flat disc floating on water and the sky a dome held up by a god called Atlas.

For years people believed the Earth was flat and that sailors could sail over the edge into the mouths of monsters.

Some sailors believed that to cross the world they had to sail through the fire zone, where the sea boiled and the land burned.

We know now that we live on a round ball spinning in space. Nobody falls off because the force of gravity holds us on.

Why not stay at home?

One reason why people risked their lives to explore the Earth was to have adventures.

OTHER EXPLORERS, SUCH AS THE VENETIAN, MARCO POLO, WISHED TO DO TRADE WITH FAR AWAY LANDS.

CHRISTOPHER COLUMBUS WANTED TO FIND A NEW SEA ROUTE TO INDIA. HE SAILED OFF COURSE. INSTEAD, HE FOUND AMERICA.

HERNANDO CORTES, A SPANISH EXPLORER, FOUGHT THE AZTECS IN MEXICO FOR THEIR GOLD AND LAND.

DAVID LIVINGSTONE SPENT MANY YEARS IN AFRICA, SEARCHING FOR THE SOURCE OF THE RIVER NILE

CAPTAIN SCOTT RACED AMUNDSEN TO THE SOUTH POLE. HE LOST THE RACE AND DIED ON HIS WAY BACK.

Finding the way

Explorers need to know in which direction they are going. Long ago they used to pick up clues from things around them.

They looked for the Pole star to find north and south. They watched where the Sun rose and set to find east and west.

The winds and sea currents helped explorers to find their way. They also looked out for birds flying towards land.

They measured the height of the sun and how high the stars were above the horizon to find out where they were.

From this they could work out their latitude (how far north or south they were) and longitude (how far east or west).

Explorers now use a compass to find their way. The needle always points north and the other directions are marked.

Finding the way back

Explorers have to be able to find their way back home and show other people how to follow in their footsteps.

They draw maps which show the shape of the land, how far it is from one place to another and how to get there.

Nowadays there are all sorts of maps. They are often coloured and have picture symbols to show where different things are.

The colours and symbols mean different things on different maps, so each map has a key to explain what they stand for.

Over the centuries people have explored most of the Earth and have put together the map of the world that we use today.

People still go on exploring but these days the only unknown places left are the depths of the oceans and Outer Space.

Africa

There are six continents on the Earth. This is the continent of Africa. More than 429 million people live there and between them they speak about a thousand different languages. Until recently most of Africa was ruled by European countries but now most of the countries are run by the Africans themselves.

Where Africa is in the world

African countries

1 Gambia
2 Guinea-Bissau
3 Equatorial Guinea
4 Rwanda
5 Burundi
6 Swaziland
7 Lesotho
8 Djibouti
9 Comoros
10 Central African Republic

Ethiopian Highlands

ADDIS ABABA

crop spraying

Mount Kenya

Mount Kilimanjaro

Indian Ocean

MOMBASA

NAIROBI

MOÇAMBIQUE

Madagascar

Coffee growing

KHARTOUM

Blue Nile

White Nile

Lake Victoria

KAMPALA

Masai

Mount Ruwenzori

Lake Tanganyika

Lake Nyasa

Temple of Zimbabwe

HARARE

DURBAN

JOHANNESBURG

Cotton picking

Pygmies

River Congo

LUSAKA

River Zambezi

BULAWAYO

River Limpopo

Drakensberg Mountains

Lake Chad

Mount Cameroun

Oil drilling

Victoria Falls

Bushmen

Gold mining

River Orange

Kalahari Desert

Table Mountain

LUANDA

River Niger

LAGOS

ACCRA

Ivory Coast

Harvesting cocoa nuts

TIMBUKTU

CAPE TOWN

Atlantic Ocean

E

N

S

W

27

The Americas

The Americas run from the cold lands near the North Pole to Antarctica. The largest jungles on Earth are around the River Amazon in Brazil. Most of the people in North America are descended from European immigrants. They mainly speak English. Most South Americans speak Spanish, except in Brazil, where the people speak Portugese.

Where the Americas are in the world

Arctic Ocean

Bering Sea

icebreaker ship

fur traders

Yukon River

plane dropping water to put out forest fire

iron and gold mined in this area

ice hockey

Rocky Mountains

EDMONTON

VANCOUVER

giant redwood trees

SAN FRANCISCO

SALT LAKE CITY

LOS ANGELES

WINNIPEG

cowboys minding cattle

KANSAS

DENVER

Rio Colorado

Rio Grande

Sun and Moon pyramids

GUADALAJARA

MEXICO CITY

oil wells

HOUSTON

QUEBEC

BOSTON

NEW YORK

WASHINGTON

Space rocket taking off from Cape Canaveral

Mississippi River

Appalachian Mountains

MIAMI

Lake Superior

Lake Huron

Lake Michigan

ST LOUIS

NEW ORLEANS

cotton fields

marlin boat

transatlantic liners

Atlantic Ocean

Caribbean Sea

Pacific Ocean

Angel Falls

Yanomamo
tribal home

River Amazon

Orinoco River

SALVADOR

RIO DE JANEIRO

BRASILIA

gauchos

MONTEVIDEO

BUENOS AIRES

Rio de la Plata

Andes
tin
mining

Lake
Titicaca

BOGOTA

LIMA

SANTIAGO

wheat
fields

Tierra
del
Fuego

Perito
Moreno
glacier

volcanoes Panama
Canal

banana
trees

PANAMA

N — E — S — W

American countries

Alaska

Canada

United States of America

Mexico

Columbia

Peru

Brazil

Bolivia

Argentina

1 Guatemala
2 Belize
3 El Salvador
4 Honduras
5 Nicaragua
6 Costa Rica
7 Panama
8 Cuba
9 Jamaica
10 Haiti
11 Dominican
Republic
12 The Bahamas
13 Puerto Rico
14 Barbados
15 Trinidad

16 Ecuador
17 Venezuela
18 Guyana
19 Surinam
20 French Guyana
21 Chile
22 Paraguay
23 Uruguay
24 The Falkland Islands

29

Asia

Asia is the biggest continent in the world, and makes up nearly one third of the land on Earth. Some countries in Asia are very cold and dry while others are hot and wet. Over half the people in the world live in Asia and many of them are very poor. China alone has about 980 million people, more than any other country in the world.

Where Asia is in the world

Asian countries

1 Nepal
2 Bhutan
3 Bangladesh
4 Lebanon
5 Israel
6 Jordan
7 United Arab Emirates
8 Kuwait
9 Qatar
10 Kampuchea
11 Laos
12 Thailand

Arctic Ocean

woolly mammoth found in ice here

Bering Sea

large fish factory ship

Trans-Siberian railway

Ural Mountains

Cossack Horseman

Yurt

ULAN-BATOR

Hall of Prayer, Beijing

VLADIVOSTOK

Mount Fuji

camel cart

harvesting wheat

Gobi Desert

KYOTO

TOKYO

OSAKA

Great Wall of China

planting rice

Huang Ho River

BEIJING

SHANGHAI

weaving

KABUL

Potola Palace, Lhasa

Himalayas

River Indus

DELHI

Mount Everest

Chang Jiang River

Pacific Ocean

Minarets of Hyderabad

Taj Mahal

River Ganges

River Irrawaddy

HONG KONG

HANOI

MANILA

BOMBAY

HYDERABAD

MADRAS

RANGOON

Buddhist Temple, Rangoon

BANGKOK

Mekong River

HO CHI MINH

Long house

COLOMBO

Malaysian village

SINGAPORE

Indian Ocean

JAKARTA

31

Australia and New Zealand

Australia is the largest island in the world and the smallest continent. New Zealand is nearly 2,000 km from Australia. Until about 300 years ago the only people living in these countries were the Aborigines in Australia and the Maoris in New Zealand. Since then, however, many Europeans have settled there.

New Zealand

North Island
volcanoes
AUCKLAND
WELLINGTON
South Island
Southern Alps
CHRISTCHURCH
DUNEDIN
Stewart Island
Tasman Sea
Pacific Ocean

Where Australia and New Zealand are in the world

Coral Sea
Great Barrier Reef
Pacific Ocean
Tasman Sea
Indian Ocean

BRISBANE
sheep shearing
surfing
lifeguard on patrol
Opera house
SYDNEY
CANBERRA
Australian Alps
River Murrumbidgee
River Murray
Tasmania
HOBART
MELBOURNE
ADELAIDE
Flinders Ranges
Great Australian Bight
Nullarbor Plain
Great Victoria Desert
Ayers Rock
Lake Disappointment
Gibson Desert
Great Sandy Desert
Simpson Desert
Lake Eyre
ALICE SPRING
flying doctor
bush fires
tower tree
spotting bush fires
Aborigines
food train
DARWIN
River Chamberlain
helicopter herding cattle
stilt house
sugar cane
River Flinders
iron mining
River Ashburton
River Gascoyne
River Murchison
sheep farm
KALGOORLIE
PERTH
felling eucalyptus trees
divers cray fishing

N E S W

32

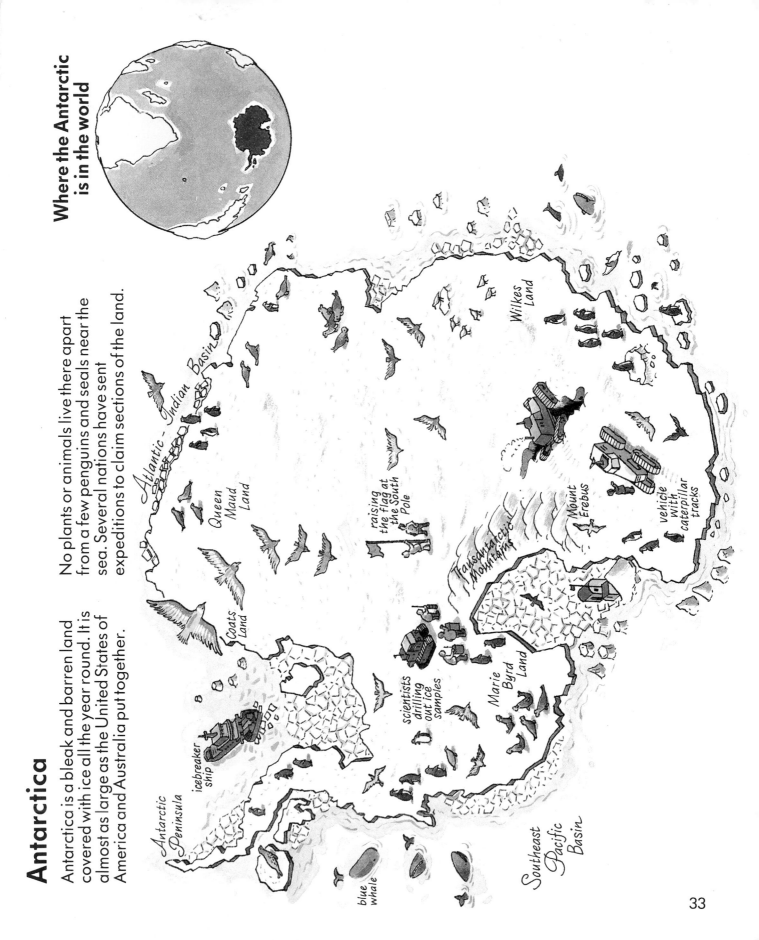

Where the Antarctic is in the world

Antarctica

Antarctica is a bleak and barren land covered with ice all the year round. It is almost as large as the United States of America and Australia put together.

No plants or animals live there apart from a few penguins and seals near the sea. Several nations have sent expeditions to claim sections of the land.

Atlantic - Indian Basin

Wilkes Land

Queen Maud Land

raising the flag at the South Pole

Mount Erebus

vehicle with caterpillar tracks

Coats Land

Transantarctic Mountains

scientists drilling out ice samples

Marie Byrd Land

icebreaker ship

Antarctic Peninsula

Southeast Pacific Basin

blue whale

33

Europe

This is the continent of Europe. It merges into Asia on its eastern side, and includes about a quarter of the USSR. Many different languages are spoken throughout Europe.

It has a mild climate, so much of its land is good for growing things. The landscape ranges from snow covered mountains to dry, hot plains. It also has some useful natural resources such as coal and iron ore.

REYKJAVIK

Where Europe is in the world

Atlantic Ocean

European countries

1 Albania
2 Andorra
3 Belgium
4 Liechtenstein
5 Luxembourg
6 Monaco
7 Netherlands
8 San Marino
9 Switzerland
10 Czechoslovakia

Iceland

Norway

Finland

Sweden

Denmark

West Germany
East Germany

USSR

Ireland

United Kingdom

Poland

Hungary

France

Austria

Romania

Portugal

Italy

Yugoslavia

Bulgaria

Spain

Greece

Turkey

STA...

Ben Nevis   Grampians

GLASGOW   EDINBURG

BELFAST

weaving linen   Pennines

DUBLIN

CARDIFF   River Thames   LOND...

English Channel

River Loire

Pyrenees

River Garo...

River Douro

River Tagus

MADRID

River Ebro

VALENCIA

Medi...

Arctic Ocean

HAMMERFEST
TROMSØ

reindeer herd

N
W   E
S

drying fish

Sauna bath

Lake Onega

TRONDHEIM
Scandinavian Mountains
drilling for iron ore

BERGEN

Baltic Sea

HELSINKI

Lake Ladoga

GORKY

Trans Siberian railway

OSLO

STOCKHOLM

MOSCOW

River Volga

KRISTIANSAND

glass blowing

ship building

NGER

th Sea

COPENHAGEN

GDANSK

River Elbe

AMSTERDAM

BERLIN

WARSAW

River Vistula

River Don

River Rhine

RUSSELS

Carpathian Mountains

River Dnieper

PRAGUE

Swiss Chalet

River Danube

Mt. Blanc

carpet making

Black Sea

MILAN

VENICE

Balkan Mountains

Rose field

ROME

Adriatic Sea

ISTANBUL

ANKARA

Mount Vesuvius

Apennines

The Bosphorus

Taurus Mountains

Mt. Etna

Aegean Sea

Parthenon

nean Sea

ATHENS

35

The Earth's story

The Earth was formed about 4,600 million years ago from gas and dust. It was so hot that it became a ball of liquid rock. As time went by its surface cooled and formed a hard crust.

Scientists think that over millions of years the shape of the land and the climate changed. Some animals died out and others appeared which could survive in the new conditions.

Where the seas came from

3,800 million years ago

The hot Earth was covered with thick clouds of steam and gas. As the temperature cooled, it began to rain. It rained for hundreds of years and the seas formed.

For the first thousand million years, there was no life on Earth. During this stormy time, mountains were formed and worn away. The land was covered by the sea and then left dry again.

Where life began

3,500-500 million years ago

The first living things on Earth were too tiny to be seen and lived in the seas.

Later, sea plants formed. They gave out oxygen, which the first sea animals needed to breathe.

Fish were the first animals with a backbone and a kind of skeleton inside their bodies.

Life in the swamps

500-280 million years ago

As more land appeared out of the seas, living things spread on to the wet land. Many plants grew there and animals could now feed on land.

Over a long period of time some types of fish developed lungs. They could breathe out of water and drag themselves along with their strong fins.

These animals, amphibians, could live both on land and in water. Along with many insects, they lived in the warm, steamy swamps covering the Earth.

Reptiles

280 million years ago

The climate on Earth grew hotter and the swamps dried up. Amphibians needed water to lay eggs, so many died out. Animals, called reptiles, developed. They laid eggs on the land and were able to live in the new conditions.

Monster reptiles, the dinosaurs, roamed the Earth. Some of them were 30 times bigger than an elephant. Many of them ate plants. Some reptiles, called pterosaurs could fly. Dinosaurs died out about 60 million years ago.

Mammals

190 million years ago

Scientists do not know exactly why the dinosaurs died out, but 150 million years before they did, the first mammals appeared on Earth.

Mammals are clever animals which feed their babies on milk. It was about this time that the first flowering plants grew.

Man and the million year winter

2 million years ago

The climate grew colder and the Ice Ages began. Much of the land was covered in thick ice and only mammals with lots of fur could survive the cold.

During the Ice Ages, some of the earliest human beings lived in caves. They lit fires to keep warm and made stone tools.

Scientists think that in 5,000 million years time the Earth will end. By then the Sun may have grown to 100 times its size and could burn up our planet.

Plants and flowers

There are over 350,000 different types of plant in the world. All living things depend on plants for their survival.

Plant power

People and animals need the oxygen which plants give off so that they can breathe.

Plants use the carbon dioxide that people and animals breathe out.

How do plants live?

Green plants make their own food. They soak up water and minerals from the soil which go up the stems to the leaves.

In the leaves, sunlight helps water and carbon dioxide from the air to make sugar. Sugar is food for plants.

Animals and people move around to find food. Plants make their own. They spend their whole lives in one place.

From seed to seed

CATERPILLARS, SLUGS AND SNAILS LIKE TO EAT YOUNG SHOOTS.

Most plants grow from seeds. A sunflower seed rests until rain makes it swell. A root grows down into the soil and a shoot pushes up towards the light.

At first the plant gets all its food from the seed, but once proper leaves grow they make food for the plant. Then the plant grows a flower bud.

The flower opens and is soon pollinated. New seeds grow, ripen and fall to the ground. Those that survive grow into flowers the following year.

Why do plants have flowers?

Flowers are important because they are the part of the plant which makes the seeds.

To make the seeds, a fine dust called pollen has to be carried from one part of a flower to another. Insects, or the wind, do this job.

Flowers produce a sweet liquid called nectar which many insects like to drink. The flowers' colour and scent draw them to the nectar.

As an insect drinks, pollen sticks to its body. When the insect visits another flower this pollen rubs off on to it and pollinates it.

How seeds leave plants

When seeds are ripe, they leave the plant to grow in a new place. Many are blown away by the wind or carried by water.

Some seeds stick to the coats or feet of birds and animals. Later on they fall off and grow where they land.

Other seeds grow inside pods which ripen in the Sun and burst open, hurling the seeds away from the parent plant.

Trappers, stranglers and pricklers

Some plants eat insects. A venus fly trap's leaves snap shut when touched by an insect.

Some plants are parasites and feed off living plants. They have no roots in the ground.

Other plants have prickles or can sting, which helps to protect them from birds or animals.

Trees and habitats

Trees cover about a third of the Earth's land surface. They are the largest living things and live longer than anything else.

The tallest tree on record is a redwood tree in America called 'Tallest Tree'. It is 112.1m high.

The oldest tree on record was a bristlecone pine in America. It was 4,900 years old when it was cut down.

Why trees lose their leaves

Trees called evergreens can keep each leaf for several years. Deciduous trees lose all their leaves every year.

Leaves use sunlight to make food for the tree. In the autumn there is not enough sunlight for the leaves to make food.

A corky layer grows across each leaf stalk. Water cannot reach the leaves, so they die. New leaves grow in the spring.

How old is a tree?

Every year a layer of wood grows inside the trunk and makes a ring. The number of rings on a tree trunk tells you how old the tree is. They also tell you the tree's life story.

6 NARROW RINGS SHOW THERE WAS A DROUGHT ONE YEAR.

1 THE WIDE EVEN RINGS MEAN THIS TREE GREW QUICKLY AT FIRST.

2 IT WAS NEARLY KNOCKED OVER, BUT GREW MORE QUICKLY ON ONE SIDE TO STRAIGHTEN ITSELF.

5 THESE ARE FIRE SCARS FROM A FOREST FIRE.

3 FOR A WHILE THE TREE WAS CROWDED BY OTHERS. THE THIN RINGS SHOW THAT THIS MADE IT GROW SLOWLY.

4 THE TREES AROUND IT WERE CUT DOWN AND THE TREE HAD MORE ROOM SO IT GREW MORE QUICKLY AGAIN.

40

The tree house

Many things can live in and around a tree. They all live alongside each other. Each of them has a place of its own so that they do not have to compete for the food and shelter a tree gives them.

BLUE TIT

Great spotted woodpeckers chip away the bark and eat the insects beneath it.

The lichen moth hides on the tree. Its wings look the same as the lichen growing on the tree trunk.

These grey squirrels live in a leafy nest, called a drey, where they rear their young.

The long-eared bat hangs in the hollow trunk and sleeps during the day.

TAWNY OWL

ACORN WEEVIL

Plants like this ivy climb up trees to get more light.

FOX AND CUBS

VIOLETS

RABBITS

TOAD

WILD BEES

SPECKLED WOOD BUTTERFLY

BADGER

HEDGEHOG

SHREW

Earthworms eat dead leaves which fall off the trees. Moles tunnel to catch the worms.

WORMS

MOLE

Insects

There are over a million different kinds of insect and they live everywhere in the world, except in deep sea water. They usually have six legs, a pair of feelers, one or two pairs of wings and a body divided into three parts.

Spiders are not insects

Spiders belong to a group of animals called arachnids. Unlike insects, they have eight legs and no wings. There are only two parts to their bodies and they usually have eight eyes.

Parts of a fly

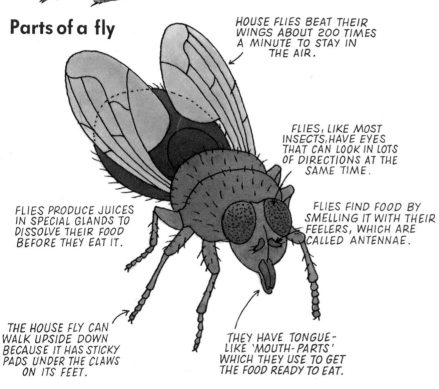

HOUSE FLIES BEAT THEIR WINGS ABOUT 200 TIMES A MINUTE TO STAY IN THE AIR.

FLIES, LIKE MOST INSECTS, HAVE EYES THAT CAN LOOK IN LOTS OF DIRECTIONS AT THE SAME TIME.

FLIES PRODUCE JUICES IN SPECIAL GLANDS TO DISSOLVE THEIR FOOD BEFORE THEY EAT IT.

FLIES FIND FOOD BY SMELLING IT WITH THEIR FEELERS, WHICH ARE CALLED ANTENNAE.

THE HOUSE FLY CAN WALK UPSIDE DOWN BECAUSE IT HAS STICKY PADS UNDER THE CLAWS ON ITS FEET.

THEY HAVE TONGUE-LIKE 'MOUTH-PARTS' WHICH THEY USE TO GET THE FOOD READY TO EAT.

Biters and suckers

Not all insects feed in the same way. Wasps and beetles can bite things and have strong jaws and sharp teeth.

Mosquitoes drink human or animal blood by sucking it up through their needle-like mouth parts. Some carry diseases.

Hide and seek

Some insects look like plants. This camouflages them so that neither their prey, nor their enemies, can see them.

Some insects mimic others to confuse their enemies. Birds leave the harmless hornet moth alone, mistaking it for the dangerous stinging hornet.

Wasps and bees have poisonous stings. They sting their enemies to defend themselves.

The four stages of a butterfly

After a female butterfly has mated, she lays her eggs on a plant and dies. A caterpillar hatches from each egg and begins to eat.

As it eats, it outgrows its skin and grows a new one. When it is fully grown, its skin hardens to form a chrysalis. Changes begin to take place inside it.

After a while, a butterfly emerges from the chrysalis. It dries its wings and flies off in search of food.

Inside the palace

A single honey bee cannot survive on its own for long. Bees live in hives along with as many as 80,000 other bees.

Every hive has one queen bee, thousands of worker bees and several hundred male bees which are called drones.

The queen bee lays all the eggs but she cannot look after them. Some of the eggs hatch into drones, whose job it is to fertilise eggs.

At first worker bees build and clean the hive.

Later they feed the grubs that emerge from the eggs. The grubs will grow into bees.

Older worker bees go out in search of nectar and pollen.

Dancing the waggle

All the bees eat honey. They make it from flower nectar and keep it in six-sided wax cells called honeycomb.

Bees dance to tell each other where to find nectar. A circular dance means it is near by. A waggle dance means it is further away.

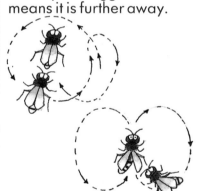

When there are too many bees in a hive, a second queen flies away with a swarm of workers and starts a new hive.

43

Life in the ocean

Life at the bottom

Many fish and other creatures live close to the rocks, mud and sand near the seashore. The shells on the beach were once the homes of soft-bodied sea creatures. Crabs search the seashore for food at high tide.

Seaweed

Sea plants do not have roots, flowers or real leaves. Some of them fasten themselves to rocks with sucker pads and grow long stems which reach towards the sunlight. Little bubbles of gas help the stems to float.

Limpets move about on a fleshy foot, but always return to the same place on a rock.

Sea anemones paralyse small fish with their tentacles, then they feed on them.

If a starfish has an arm bitten off by an enemy, it can grow a new one.

Fish facts

Many fish have good eyesight. They do not have eyelids as the sea keeps their eyes moist and clean.

Fish have a good sense of smell. They smell through their nostrils, but they do not breathe through them.

Fish use their fins for cornering, balancing, braking and steering. They use their tails to drive themselves along.

4

Food of the sea

Plankton are minute animals and plants that drift close to the surface of the water. They are the main food supply of many sea creatures.

Life on the surface

Most fish live near the surface or in the middle depths of the oceans. These fish never stop swimming. Their streamlined shapes help them swim fast.

Life in the dark

No sunlight reaches the depths of the ocean. Few fish live there and those that do often have their own lights to lure their prey and attract mates.

Sometimes there can be so much plankton in the water the sea turns green or red.

Flying fish can travel 100 metres through the air.

The enormous whale shark lives entirely on plankton.

The giant squid's enemy is the sperm whale. They do battle deep in the ocean.

Scientists thought coelacanths had died out 70 million years ago, but in 1938 one was found alive and well.

Like people, fish need oxygen to breathe, but they get it from water. As a fish swallows, water passes over its gills.

The gills strain the oxygen from the water and then force it out through gill covers behind the fish's eyes.

Most fish have babies by laying eggs. Some of them build nests but others lay them straight into the water.

Reptiles

Alligators, crocodiles, tortoises, turtles, snakes and lizards are all members of the reptile family.

Reptiles live mainly on land, but some of them spend a lot of time in water. They all have scaly, watertight skins.

They are cold-blooded which means that the temperature of their bodies is always the same as that of their surroundings.

Reptiles are carnivorous. This means that they eat other animals. Some of them can swallow their prey whole.

Reptiles lay eggs

After she has mated, the female crocodile digs a hole at night and lays about forty eggs. Both parents guard them carefully.

In about 90 days the young crocodiles hatch. Crocodiles carry their babies around in their jaws to keep them safe.

The babies can feed themselves straightaway, but their parents still keep watch over them until they are really strong.

Dealing with enemies

Some snakes kill their prey with a poisonous bite. Others, such as the boa constrictor, squeeze their prey to death.

Tortoises and turtles draw back into the safety of their hard shells if they are frightened or in any kind of danger.

Some lizards have tails that break off when they want to escape from an enemy. A new tail grows in its place.

Amphibians

What is an amphibian?

Frogs, toads, newts, salamanders and worm-like animals, called caecilians, are all types of amphibian.

They are called amphibians because they live both in water and on land. They only need water to breed in.

Amphibians have backbones and are cold-blooded. Most of them breathe through their skins, but some have lungs.

Frogs

Like all amphibians, frogs lay their eggs in water. The eggs are called 'frog spawn' and look like tiny balls of jelly.

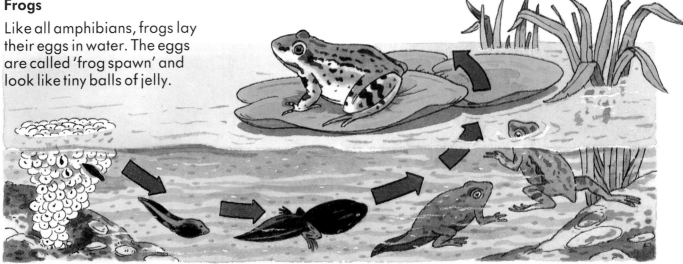

After about two weeks tadpoles hatch. They eat with their horny lips and teeth, and breathe through tiny gills, like fish.

Two small bumps appear on their tails which grow into back legs. At about ten weeks old, tadpoles grow forelegs and their tails become shorter.

Now they are tiny frogs which can leap out of the water and breathe air. Every day they hunt for insects to eat.

Other amphibians

The fire salamander has a deadly form of protection. It oozes poison from its skin to warn animals not to eat it.

An axolotl is a type of salamander. Unlike most other amphibians, it breeds and spends its whole life in water.

Some toads that live in the Australian desert survive in dry weather by storing rainwater in their bodies.

Birds

What are birds?

There are about 8,600 different kinds of bird in the world. Birds are warm-blooded, like us. They have backbones and are the only creatures with feathers.

All birds have wings and most of them can fly. Birds which cannot fly, such as the African ostrich, have strong legs so that they can run fast to escape from their enemies.

How do birds fly?

A wing can bend just like an arm. Birds twist or bend their wings to change direction in the air.

Birds are very light because their bones are hollow and full of air. Their streamlined shapes help them to fly fast.

When birds take off, they leap into the air and flap their wings very quickly.

Some birds are so heavy they have to run and flap their wings to get up enough speed before they can take off.

Large birds spread their wings and flap them slowly. They glide on currents of air, searching the ground for food.

Small birds flap their wings fast. The hummingbird beats its wings so fast it can hover, fly backwards or forwards.

Migrating birds

Some birds migrate. This means they fly away to a warm place every autumn where there is plenty of food to eat.

Some birds fly by day and others by night. They use the Sun, stars and landmarks to help them find their way.

Arctic terns fly the greatest distance. They fly across the world from the Arctic to the Antarctic and back each year.

Beaks and birds of prey

Birds cannot chew because they have no teeth. They swallow their food whole. It is ground up in a part of their stomach, called the gizzard.

You can tell what a bird eats by the shape of its beak. Pelicans catch fish in their baggy beaks. Flamingoes can sieve food out of mud with their beaks.

Birds of prey have curved talons which they use to stun and grab small animals and birds. They have large, hooked beaks for tearing up the flesh.

Feathers

Feathers are much warmer than fur. Birds fluff up their feathers on cold days to help them keep as warm as possible.

Birds clean, tidy and oil their feathers. The oil comes from a gland above the tail and keeps the feathers waterproof.

Feathers become ragged and worn after a while. At least once a year they drop out, or moult, and new ones grow.

Nesting

Male birds have to attract a mate. Some birds have one partner for life. Others find a new mate every nesting season.

Some birds show off their colours or preen their feathers to attract a mate. Others put on a flying display or perform dances.

All birds lay eggs, usually in a hidden nest. The female bird, and sometimes the male, sits on the eggs to keep them warm.

Chicks hatched in nests above the ground are usually naked and helpless. Their parents feed them until they can fly properly.

Chicks hatched on the ground are often covered with fluffy down. They can run and peck things to eat when they hatch.

Mammals

There are about 4,500 kinds of mammals. All the animals on these pages are mammals. So are human beings.

Mammals are the only animals with hair or fur. Some grow a thicker, warmer coat in the cold winter months.

Mammals are warm-blooded. This means that their bodies stay the same temperature when the weather is hot or cold.

Moving about

Most land mammals have four legs. Sea mammals, such as sea-lions and dolphins, have flippers instead of legs.

Some mammals, such as kangaroos, hop about on their hind legs which are very strong. Their tails help them to balance.

Bats are the only mammals which can fly. They use their arms as wings. The skin is stretched over the bones.

Protection

Mammals protect themselves from danger in different ways. Some of them can run away fast. Others have prickly coats to protect them. The skunk makes a nasty smell.

Many jungle and forest mammals have markings on their coats to camouflage them from both their enemies and prey. They match the colours and patterns on the trees.

Living together

Some mammals, such as chimpanzees, are very sociable and live together in groups. The females look after the young and the males defend the group from their enemies.

Lions live in a group called a pride. The lionesses do most of the hunting and feed and care for the cubs. The male lions keep watch over the pride's territory.

Mammals are the only animals which feed their new-born babies with milk. Some feed lots of babies at once.

Many mammals are intelligent and curious. They can learn how to do new and different things.

All of them breathe air. Even a whale, which spends its whole life in water, comes to the surface to breathe.

Most mammals build homes to keep them dry, safe and warm. Some of them spend the whole winter asleep in their homes, such as the polar bear, which digs a cave out of snow and ice.

Beavers build their homes in rivers and streams with sticks and mud. Their homes, called lodges, have underwater entrances. They have separate living and sleeping areas.

Baby mammals

Many mammals have more than one mate. Each year male red deer mate with a group of females.

Some babies take longer than others to grow inside their mothers. Mice take three weeks, human babies take nine months.

When they are born, baby mammals feed on their mother's milk. This has everything the baby needs to grow.

Some mothers stay with their babies for longer than others. They all stay until the babies can look after themselves.

Baby kangaroos are born before they are fully formed. They finish growing inside their mother's warm pouch.

The platypus and the spiny anteater are two unusual mammals as they lay eggs. Their eggs have soft shells.

The human body

How do we stand up?

There are about 206 bones in the human body. They are all joined together to make a skeleton. Without this you would just be a mound of flesh.

Bones protect vital parts of the body, such as the heart and lungs, from damage. The brain is protected by 30 skull bones all tightly locked together.

How bones are joined together

A joint is where two bones meet. Most bones move at the joint. Some move backwards and forwards like a hinge.

Joints contain a fluid which keeps them oiled and easy to move. Straps, called ligaments, hold the bones in place.

Others are called ball and socket joints. These allow the bones to move in many different directions.

Some people can bend their joints more than other people because they have very loose ligaments.

Why you can move

You can move because your bones are attached to muscles. Every joint has two muscles which work in turn.

Overworked muscles produce a poison which makes you feel tired. Blood washes it away and you feel better.

To make a bone move, a message from your brain tells one muscle to tighten up and the other to relax.

Your heart is another type of muscle. It works by itself without stopping for the whole of your life.

What happens to the food you eat?

You grind up food with your teeth and it mixes with saliva in your mouth. This helps it to slide down to your stomach.

Special juices in your stomach break the food down into tiny bits. This is called digestion.

The food enters the blood stream through a wiggly tube called the small intestine, and goes all around your body.

Waste goes into a tube, called the large intestine, and gets ready to leave the body. Other waste is removed as blood passes through the kidneys.

How blood goes round

Your heart is a pump. It pumps blood out through one tube and sucks it in through another.

Blood flows around your body through rubbery tubes. Laid end to end, they would go nearly half way to the moon.

Tubes called arteries take blood away from the heart. It turns red when it collects oxygen from the lungs.

Used blood returns to the heart in tubes called veins. It looks purple because the oxygen has been used up.

What does blood do?

Blood carries tiny bits of food to your liver. The liver sorts the food out so that it is ready for your body to use.

Blood carries the oxygen you breathe in around your body. It takes waste gas to your lungs for you to breathe out.

Your blood fights germs that get into your body and could make you ill. It surrounds them and then kills them.

When you hurt yourself, your blood makes special gluey stuff which blocks wounds and stops them bleeding.

The human body

What happens when you breathe?

You can live for several days without food and water but only a few minutes without air.

Your body uses oxygen from the air. Blood vessels carry the oxygen from your lungs into your bloodstream.

The air you breathe in goes down your windpipe into your two lungs. Lungs are full of tiny holes, like sponges.

Any dirt you breathe in is trapped by tiny hairs in your nose so that it does not reach your lungs.

How do lungs work?

As you breathe in, your ribs move up and out. A muscle under your lungs, called the diaphragm, flattens down. Air rushes in to fill your lungs.

When you breathe out, your ribs drop back. Your diaphragm pops up. All the used gases are squeezed out.

Making sense

You have five senses. These take messages to your brain telling you what is happening to your body. Your memory helps to work out what they mean.

Hearing

When your ears hear this sound your memory says 'music'.

Sight

Your eyes see the clock and your memory says '7.30'.

Smell

Your nose smells cooking and your memory says ' cake'.

Taste

Your tongue tastes the drink and your memory says 'milk'.

Touch

You feel with the skin on your fingers. Your memory works out who or what it is.

Brain work

Your brain is like a busy control room. It receives and sends out lots of messages to the rest of your body. Different parts of your brain do different jobs.

This part receives important messages from your five senses and works out what to do. It shuts out any messages that are not important.

Your memory sorts out important messages from your senses and stores them away. It also works out what the messages mean.

This part keeps your body going. It makes you breathe and your heart beat. It works all the time, even when you are asleep.

All messages go through here. In an emergency, it calls for action. It wakes you up and gets you ready to run or fight.

This cord inside your spine is the main path for messages travelling between your brain and the rest of your body.

Lines, called nerves, carry messages from the spinal cord to your muscles. Nerves also carry messages from your senses to your brain.

55

Looking after the land

Rainforests cover an area about the size of the United States. More than half the world's types of animals and birds live in these forests.

But thousands of them all over the world are in danger of dying out because the rainforests are being cut down and destroyed by Man.

People chop down the trees so that they can sell the valuable wood for money. Others clear the land to grow crops for food.

When forests are cut and burnt, the animals and birds lose their homes and food. If there are no other trees to move to, they starve and die.

Making deserts

Many people clear forests to grow grass for their cattle. If the animals eat all the grass the land becomes desert.

The loss of the forests is likely to alter the world's climate, causing droughts and changes in wind and rainfall.

Many of the things we use come from rainforests, such as medicines, rubber, oils, spices and perfumes.

Poisoning the Earth

People destroy plants, birds and animals when they tip poisonous wastes, such as oil into rivers, lakes and seas.

Untreated animal and human sewage is often tipped on to the land and into the water, helping to spread diseases.

Waste gases from factories and car exhausts pollute the air. They make it harmful to breathe and kill plants and trees.

Farming the land

Soil is full of minerals and elements that plants need to grow. Without these things the land is bare and lifeless.

If soil is overused, healthy plants cannot grow in it. Good farmers feed the soil with the minerals their crops use up.

Not all plants use up the same things from the soil. Farmers give the soil a rest by growing different crops each season.

Tree roots help to keep the soil in place. They stop it from being blown away by the wind or washed away by the rain.

Some farmers build terrace walls to stop steep land from slipping away and to make more flat land for them to farm.

Others plant hedges around fields to protect the land from wind. Many birds and animals make their homes in hedges.

A safe life in the wild

Many countries set up nature reserves where animals can live safely in their natural habitat. People can visit them there.

Wildlife moves to town

A few animals, such as foxes, have moved from their natural home in the country to towns, where food is easier to find.

The story of people

Millions of years ago

Our early ancestors were probably ape-like creatures who were much smaller than us.

About four million years ago these early people began to walk upright and communicate with each other.

They ate plants, berries and raw animal meat, and the first tools they used were made from sharpened stones.

Wandering hunters

40,000BC

These people lived in caves and hunted animals with stone weapons. They learned to use fire to cook and keep warm.

Village farmers

10,000BC

In the Middle East people collected wild seeds and grew crops. The first farm animals were tamed wild animals.

The people built mud houses and settled down to farm the land. They made clay pots and learned how to weave cloth.

The first cities

5000BC to 2000BC

The Sumerians in the Middle East built villages which grew into huge walled cities. They had a temple in the centre.

The Sumerians used wheels and were skilled metal workers. They were one of the first peoples to write things down.

The Ancient World

3100BC to 1500BC

500BC to 140BC

The Ancient Egyptians used a calendar like ours. They designed the water clock and could make paper. Their kings, called pharaohs, were often buried in pyramids when they died.

The Ancient Greeks were great sculptors, writers and doctors. Greek citizens were the first people to help govern their cities by voting on important matters.

750BC to AD500

The Romans had very large armies. They conquered Europe, North Africa, and the Middle East.

Their engineers built fine roads and bridges across the Empire. They also built many towns and cities, and set up trade routes.

Dates with BC after them are the number of years before the birth of Christ counting backwards. Dates with AD are number of years after the birth of Christ.

BC ⟷ AD

The Middle Ages

AD1000 to AD1450

In the Middle Ages each of the different countries of Europe was ruled by a king or emperor who owned all the land.

When the king wanted money or soldiers, he met his most important subjects. This idea led to the first parliament.

Clues to the past

For thousands of years different people have lived on the same site, leaving behind all sorts of remains. Scientists dig these up to discover clues to our history.

The Renaissance

AD1450 to AD1750

This was the time when Europeans began to take a great interest in art and learning.

They did lots of scientific experiments to find out more about the world around them.

The Industrial Revolution ## Modern times

AD1750 to AD1914

New machines were invented which did many of the jobs people used to do by hand.

Electronic inventions have changed people's lives much faster than ever before.

A living thing, such as a tree, absorbs radioactive carbon or C14. When it dies C14 slowly leaves its wood. Scientists can work out how old the wood is from the amount of C14 left.

You can read more about some of these people on pages 60 to 71.

Cavemen

Our direct ancestors were cave people, called Cromagnons, who lived between 35,000 and 12,000 years ago, at the end of the last Ice Age.

Cromagnons hunted animals, caught fish and collected nuts, seeds and berries to eat. Their weapons were made of flint and bone.

Tent life

Some groups hunted away from the caves on the bare, frozen plains of Eastern Europe. They lived in tents.

The tents were made of animal skins, raised over shallow pits with low stone walls. Bones or tusks held them up.

A large tent could house several families. Each family had its own fireplace for heating and cooking.

Dressing up

Cromagnons were the first people to sew. They made clothes by stitching skins together with bone needles.

Sometimes they decorated their clothes with little beads of coloured rock or shells with holes in them.

They wore necklaces and bracelets made of teeth, beads, ivory and stone threaded together with leather strips.

Decorating the cave

Cromagnons painted pictures of hunts on their cave walls. Their paints were made from rocks ground into powder.

To give themselves light, these early people used lamps of burning fur or moss, soaked in animal fat.

They carved stone pictures of very fat, or pregnant women. This may have been to bring them good fortune.

Preparing for the hunt

The hunters made their axes, knives and spears out of pieces of flint which they chipped into shape and sharpened.

They dipped animal leg bones into boiling water to soften and straighten them so they could be used as spears.

Sometimes they made traps. They dug pits, filled them with sharpened stakes, then covered them with branches.

The kill

The greatest prey of all for the Cromagnon hunters was the giant woolly mammoth, as it provided them with everything they needed.

They would hunt the mammoth down and then close in for the kill with their spears. Sometimes they would drive it into a bog, so it could not fight back easily.

The hunters skinned the mammoth, and carried pieces of meat and bones back to the camp.

If a wounded hunter died, he was buried in the floor of the cave with his jewellery and weapons.

Then they covered him with red ochre powder and laid mammoth bones or flowers on his grave.

61

The Ancient Egyptians

The Ancient Egyptians lived between the years 4000BC and 500BC, in the dry, hot country along the River Nile.

Every July the river flooded and the farmers grew their crops in the rich, fertile mud which the flood left behind.

It was a serious crime either to block the channels of water to a farmer's field, or to move his boundary stones.

A RICH NOBLE LIVED IN THIS HOUSE MADE OF SUN DRIED MUD BRICKS, WITH A WOODEN ROOF.

THE WALLS AND MUD FLOORS WERE PAINTED AND OFTEN HUNG WITH REED MATS.

THE FAMILY SLEPT AT THE BACK, OR IN THE SUMMER, ON THE ROOF. THEY HAD A BATHROOM AND A LAVATORY.

Cool clothes and make-up

Egyptians wore cool clothes made of linen. The men wore short tunics and the women long tunics with shoulder straps.

Both men and women wore make-up. Rich people wore wigs and jewellery made from gold and semi-precious stones.

The children often did not wear clothes. Boys had shaved heads with a single lock of hair, and girls wore several plaits.

Feasts and fun

Rich people had grand parties with lots of food and drink, served by servants and slaves.

A cone of scented fat was put on each guest's head. As it melted, it covered them with scent.

The guests were entertained by singers, dancers, acrobats, jugglers and musicians.

Sports and games

The Egyptians hunted on land from chariots and in water from boats. Here they are catching a hippopotamus with harpoons and ropes.

The children played with leather balls and toys made of wood and ivory. They enjoyed wrestling and fencing with wooden swords.

Education

Most children did not go to school. Boys learned their father's trade and girls helped their mothers.

Rich children had a tutor or went to school. They learned to read and write on paper made from papyrus reeds.

They used picture writing called hieroglyphs. Sometimes a picture stood for a sound and several pictures made a word.

The burial of a king

Egyptian kings built huge stone pyramids in the desert as their burial places.

Men spent part of each year working on buildings for the king, as a tax payment.

When the king died, his body was preserved and wrapped in linen. This was called a mummy.

The king was buried seventy days after death. His funeral procession included priests, priestesses and paid mourners.

Inside the tomb were clothes, weapons, furniture and anything else the king needed for his life after death.

Sometimes robbers would try to break into the sealed tomb and steal the treasures which were buried with the king.

The Ancient Romans

The Ancient Romans lived between about 750BC and AD500. Rome grew up from villages built on seven hills near the River Tiber.

Romans were either citizens or non-citizens. Citizens had certain rights, such as a say in the government, and were protected by laws.

Many Romans had slaves. As the Roman Empire grew, thousands of prisoners were taken and sold at slave markets.

A Roman street

Most Romans rented rooms in blocks of flats. Many did not have kitchens because of the danger of catching fire.

In Rome there were several markets. Other towns just had one which was held once a week in the main square.

Water was piped into the city and Romans collected it from public fountains. Underground pipes carried away the waste.

People bought hot food and drink from eating houses and street stalls. They drank wine and talked in the taverns.

The shops opened on to the street and had a counter at the front. Slaves often did the shopping for their owners.

Pavements were built higher than the roads. People used stepping stones to cross the road in wet weather.

Only rich people could afford a house. They stuck tiles on the floor to make pictures, called mosaics, and painted the walls.

Wealthy Romans lay on couches for meals. They used their fingers to eat from big dishes. Some of them went on eating until they were sick.

Washing and dressing

Roman citizens liked to visit the public baths. The steam baths and hot pools were heated by an underground furnace. They also played games and met their friends there.

Men who were citizens wore a tunic and a piece of cloth wrapped round their body, called a toga. The women wore a dress called a stola, with a shawl over the top.

School and play

Only the children of rich parents went to school. Some were taught at home by private tutors or educated slaves. They learnt to write on wax tablets and used an abacus for arithmetic.

Keeping fit was important, so when lessons were over, the boys ran, wrestled and fenced. Boys and girls liked to play games such as rolling hoops and throwing knuckle bones.

The Roman army

The army was very well trained and conquered a great deal of land for the Roman Empire. So the Roman way of life spread.

When attacking the enemy, the army used catapults that hurled heavy rocks, and battering rams to knock down the walls.

Roman foot soldiers were each given a bronze helmet, a shield, breastplate, short sword and a long spear.

Games

On public holidays or to celebrate a victory, great fights and chariot races were held to entertain everyone.

Men, called gladiators, were taught to fight and die bravely. They were often slaves, criminals or men in debt.

Some men fought wild animals. The crowd decided if the loser should live or die, by putting their thumbs up or down.

The Middle Ages

Between about AD1000 and AD1450 each country in Europe was ruled by a king who owned all the land.

The king gave land to the most important men, the nobles. In return they promised to obey him and fight for him.

Workers, called villeins, farmed the noble's land and paid him rent in money, crops, or by working for him.

Castle life

Kings and nobles built castles to protect themselves against their enemies. Armed soldiers kept watch day and night.

Training to be a knight

A noble's son trained to be a knight. First he was a pageboy in a noble's family. They taught him how to behave well.

Next he was a squire, the servant of a knight, and he learned about armour, weapons and riding.

Sometimes the lord held feasts in the great hall. All the family and important guests sat at the top table.

Minstrels played music to the guests. Often leftover food was collected and given to the local poor people.

A squire was made a knight by his lord when he had proved he was brave. Knights were called 'Sir'.

Village life

Most people lived in villages. Their small houses had thatched roofs with a hole in, to let the smoke out.

The people worked in the fields every day except on holy days and on Sundays, when they went to the village church.

Villagers could graze their cattle on 'common land'. Stray animals were locked up until their owners paid a fine.

Women spun wool from their sheep and sold it to travelling merchants who then had it woven into cloth.

If a person committed a small crime they were put in 'the stocks' as punishment and the villagers threw things at them.

Fun at the fair

When a fair came to the village, the villagers could buy the goods on sale there.

Tinkers sold pots and pans. Jugglers and musicians entertained the crowd.

The Black Death

In AD 1348 some sailors arrived in Italy, from Asia, with a terrible disease called the Black Death.

The disease spread across Europe carried by the fleas on rats. About one person in every three died of it.

The runaway villein

A villein who wanted his freedom had to run away from the village and avoid being caught for a year and a day.

If he went to a town he could learn a trade. He had to work for several years as apprentice to a craftsman.

The Industrial Revolution

The time between 1750 and 1914 is called the Industrial Revolution. This is because so many machines were invented which changed people's lives.

Before that time there were few big towns. Most people lived in the countryside. They farmed their own land or worked for the local landowner.

Some people made money from spinning and weaving wool in their homes. They sold it to travelling merchants.

The power of machines

Clever men invented machines which made cloth very quickly, and a steam engine which could drive machinery.

Factories were built for the new machines. Many people left the country and moved to the towns to work in the factories.

Coal was needed to run the machines. Children worked in the mines, hauling coal to the surface on underground rails.

The daily grind

Both children and adults worked in the factories for six days a week. The work was hard and the hours were very long.

They often worked from six in the morning till eight at night. They were paid very little and the work was sometimes dangerous.

Life in the towns

The factory owners became very rich and lived well, but the factory workers were very poor. They lived in tiny, crowded houses with no bathroom or clean water.

People who lost their jobs often had to go and live in the 'workhouse' where they were given food and a bed in return for work. Families were separated and life was hard.

Room for improvement

At last laws were made to improve people's lives. Better houses were built and free schools set up for all children.

Factories were made safer places in which to work. The working day was shortened. The jobless were given money.

Workers joined together to form trade unions, so they could bargain for better wages and working conditions.

Going further faster

Roads and bridges were built so that people and goods could move about more easily. Everyone paid a small fee, called a toll, to use them.

People realised that it was cheaper to move heavy goods, such as coal, by boat. So a huge network of canals was built.

The new steam trains carried people and goods further and faster than ever before. More families went away on holiday.

There was more trade between countries around the world as travel by steam ships became more reliable, faster and cheaper.

Modern times

The way people live and travel has changed far more over the last hundred years than ever before in history.

Two world wars caused social changes. Women now have the right to vote, and many do jobs that only men did in the past.

Modern medicine and better living conditions mean that people live longer today then they used to in the past.

Vast networks of roads, railways, ships and aeroplanes link all the world's countries.

Space probes explore the universe and send information back to Earth.

THE UNITED STATES OF AMERICA HAS ENOUGH ROAD TO GO AROUND THE WORLD NEARLY 153 TIMES.

IN 1969, NEIL ARMSTRONG, AN AMERICAN ASTRONAUT, WAS THE FIRST PERSON TO WALK ON THE MOON.

JUMBO JETS FLY FROM BRITAIN TO AUSTRALIA IN ABOUT 20 HOURS. SAILING SHIPS TOOK SIX MONTHS.

Keeping in touch

News often took weeks or months to reach people in the past. Now they receive news by television, radio and newspapers every day.

Many satellites orbit the earth. They flash information, television pictures and thousands of telephone calls all around the world.

Fast food and gadgets

Many people do their shopping in giant supermarkets. The food is often already weighed, measured and wrapped.

Refrigerators keep food fresh. Food can be deep frozen so that it can travel long distances and be sold all over the world.

Housework is much easier and faster than ever before because of the many electrical gadgets people can buy to help them.

City life

About a third of the people in the world live in towns and cities. Most cities have very tall buildings because of the shortage of land.

Machine work

Machines now do a lot of the work that people used to do.

This robot has arms that can piece things together on a factory production line.

Computers are programmed to copy human thinking. They can solve some problems faster than a person.

Pupils use machines such as computers, tape recorders, calculators and videos to help them learn.

Fame and fortune

Musicians and film stars can become world famous overnight as their records, videos and films are sold all around the world.

Every four years the best athletes in the world compete against each other at the Olympic Games to try to beat world records.

People around the world

There are many different races of people all over the world. Each race has its own customs, culture and religion.

Nowadays, fast modern travel has made it easy for people from different countries to meet and learn about each other.

Tallest, shortest and last

The tallest people in the world are the African Watussi tribe. Most of the men are over 183 cms.

Different races of people have different looks and build. They probably developed these to help them survive in the part of the world in which they live.

People living in cloudy climates may originally have had pale skins. This helped them to get the vitamins they needed from the Sun.

The smallest people also live in Africa. The Mbuti pygmies, from Zaire, are only about 132 cms.

The last primitive tribe to be discovered was in the Philippines in 1971. They lived like Stone Age people.

Black skin probably helped protect people from the Sun in hot, dry places.

People who originally lived in freezing cold conditions may have develped narrow eyes to protect them from the cold.

There are about 5,000 million people in the world. About 140 babies are born every minute of the day.

Languages

People are different from animals because they are able to speak to each other.

Learning to speak

Usually the first language a person learns to speak is called their 'mother' tongue or 'native' tongue.

In countries where many languages are spoken, there is usually one official language which is used in the schools.

700 MILLION MANDARIN   316 MILLION ENGLISH

China's official language is Mandarin. Nearly 700 million people speak it, which is more than any other language.

Language families

There are 10,000 different languages. Many of them came from a single language.

If a language is related to another it belongs to the same 'language' family.

FRENCH, SPANISH AND ITALIAN ALL GREW FROM THE LATIN LANGUAGE.

FRENCH   SPANISH

LATIN

ITALIAN

Some Eastern languages, such as Japanese, are completely different from any other.

Spreading the word

As groups of people moved from one part of the world to another, they took their language with them. In time they began to say old words in a slightly different way.

They made up new words for foreign things that they had never seen before.

Gradually a language may change so much that it becomes a new one.

73

Houses and homes

All over the world, people build houses for shelter and protection. They use materials that are easy to come by.

The African bushmen build their huts with grass and branches which they collect from the land around them.

People also build houses to suit the climate. In hot, wet places, houses are built on stilts to keep them cool and dry.

Some people live in homes which suit their lifestyle. Nomads carry tents to live in as they wander from place to place.

Sometimes homes are built to fit the space available. In big cities people live in thousands of flats in high rise blocks.

People experiment with new types of houses. This inflatable home is useful in emergencies such as a flood or earthquake.

Houses in the heat

Many villages in Africa, such as these Nabdam houses in northern Ghana, are built of mud baked hard by the Sun. The thick walls block out the Sun and keep the inside cool. The houses are painted on the outside with vegetable juices.

In the steamy Amazon jungle, Yanamo Indians build huge circular roofs with palm tree leaves laid over wooden poles. As there are no walls, they store their few belongings off the ground to keep them dry.

Houses in the cold

In Switzerland, houses called chalets are built of wood. The ground floor is made of stone which does not rot in the damp, and the windows have double layers of glass. Snow settles on the sloping roof and helps to keep the heat in.

Nowadays in Lapland most people live in small towns beyond the Arctic Circle. However, there are some reindeer herdsmen who live in tents. These are made from large branches covered in reindeer skins.

A travelling house

The Bedouins are Arabs who wander across the Arabian desert herding their animals.

They live in goat hair tents woven by the women. Each tent has a dividing curtain.

On one side the family sleep and cook. On the other, men hold meetings and meet guests.

A floating house

Many people in China cook, eat and sleep on houseboats called sampans. They also keep chickens and grow vegetables on board.

Living together

A kibbutz is a type of village in Israel where everyone shares in the work and land, and has a say in how things are organized.

Food and cooking

Everything you eat and drink affects your body in some way. Food is vital as it gives you energy to keep going. Without food you would not be able to grow, move about, keep warm or get better when you are ill. You need lots of different sorts of food to stay healthy.

People can survive for several weeks without food but die in a few days without water.

PROTEIN FOODS, SUCH AS MEAT, FISH AND MILK BUILD YOUR BODY.

VEGETABLES, FRUIT AND MILK PROVIDE THE IMPORTANT VITAMINS AND MINERALS YOUR BODY NEEDS.

STARCHY FOODS SUCH AS BREAD AND CEREALS GIVE YOU ENERGY.

YOUR BODY CAN STORE FATS FROM BUTTER AND OILS AND USE THEM LATER FOR ENERGY.

Feast or famine?

Nearly half the people in the world do not have enough food. Many people starve if drought or floods destroy their crops.

There is enough food in the world for everybody, but the great problem is sending it to where it is most needed.

Eating too much, and eating too many fatty and sugary foods can make people overweight, unhealthy and even ill.

Fast foods

Fast foods are quick and cheap to cook. Some contain a lot of fat and sugar and are bad for you if you eat too much of them.

Why do people cook?

Cooked food is easier for your stomach to digest than raw food. Cooking kills the germs that may make people ill, and makes food keep longer.

Everyday food

The main food of a country is called its 'staple' food. Rice is the staple food of half the world. It only grows in warm climates.

The biggest meal in the world

Roast camel stuffed with sheep, chickens, fish and eggs is the largest meal in the world. It is served at Bedouin weddings in Africa.

Meals around the world

This Indian family roasts meat, such as lamb or chicken, in a clay oven called a tandoor. The name 'tandoori' is given to meat dishes cooked this way. Most Indians do not eat beef.

They serve their meat with vegetables, pickles, and bread called chapattis, and eat it with their fingers. Spices are used to flavour the food and make it tasty.

Chinese families cook their food over a fire in shallow metal pans, called woks. They eat rice with vegetables and a little meat.

The food is eaten out of small bowls using wooden sticks, called chopsticks. They drink milkless tea with their meals.

This Italian family begins a meal with a plate of pasta served with a sauce. Italians eat a lot of pasta, which they make in different shapes with wheat flour and water.

Next, they have meat and vegetables, which they eat with knives and forks. They drink wine with their meal. The children drink a little wine mixed with water.

Sport

People of all ages enjoy sport. Some people like restful sports and others prefer to be active or competitive.

Plenty of exercise keeps people healthy. Swimming is a sport that exercises the muscles all over your body.

There are different ways of playing sport. Some sports, such as archery, are played by one person.

Other sports, such as tennis are played in pairs or foursomes.

Team sports, such as football, teach people to work together towards winning a goal.

Playing for fun and money

A person who plays sport only for fun is called an amateur. A person who is paid to compete and earns his living from sport, is called a professional.

What is the most popular sport?

Football is played all over the world. It began in England in the Middle Ages when people from different villages played in the streets and is now enjoyed by millions of people.

The hero's race

A marathon is a 42.195km running race. The first marathon was run by a Greek soldier in 490BC. He ran to deliver news of a victory over the Persians, but then later died of exhaustion.

The first Olympic Games

DISCUS

JAVELIN

The Ancient Greeks held games every four years. Women were not allowed to take part or watch them. Sports, such as throwing the discus and javelin, date back to these games.

The modern Olympic Games

The Olympic Games are held every four years in a different country. Amateur athletes from all around the world compete in them.

The Olympic torch is carried by runners from Athens, in Greece, to the opening ceremony. It is kept burning until the games are over.

Nowadays both women and men athletes compete in over twenty different sports and games. They are watched by millions on television.

Each winner receives a gold medal, those who come second have silver medals and people who come third are given bronze medals.

The oldest sports

Norwegian rock paintings show that people skied on snow as long ago as the Stone Age.

Over 5,000 years ago, men trained for battle with fighting sports, such as wrestling.

Animal sports

In some sports, such as show jumping, people and animals compete together.

Some people shoot animals and birds for fun. These are called 'blood' sports.

New sports

New inventions led to many new sports, such as flying, hang-gliding and motor racing.

The first motor race was held on a course between Paris and Rouen in France in 1894.

79

Writing and books

One reason why people write is to keep a record of what has happened. In the past, people kept records in other ways.

North American Indians used to weave shells into belts and circles. The patterns were a record of their tribal meetings.

Peruvians tied string into knots to help record things they wanted to remember. They called each string a 'quippu'.

Who were the first people to write?

The Egyptians and Sumerians invented picture writing about 5,000 years ago. The Egyptian picture writing is called hieroglyphics.*

The Sumerians pressed with a reed pen on to a clay tablet. Later on, their picture writing changed into wedge shaped signs.

Learning the alphabet

Most of the alphabets people use today probably came from earlier picture writing.

The Roman letter 'A' may have come from the older picture sign for an ox.

People write in different directions. Chinese can be written downwards or across.

From papyrus to paper

The Egyptians wrote on paper made of flattened papyrus. They made ink from charcoal, mixed with water and glue.

Later on, people made parchment from animal skins. It was better than papyrus as they could write on both sides.

The Chinese invented paper made from the bark of mulberry trees. Arab traders brought the secret to Europe.

*You can read more about hieroglyphics on page 63.

The first books

It was not until the Middle Ages that books began to look like they do today, with covers, pages and pictures.

Monks in monasteries who learned how to write were called scribes. They copied books and decorated them beautifully.

It took a long time and a great deal of work to make these books by hand. Only rich people and churches could afford them.

Printing machines

The first printing machine was invented about 550 years ago by a German, called Johann Gutenberg. It was worked by hand.

Modern printing machines work by electricity. They print the colours one after another on paper large enough to make several pages.

The printed pages are folded so they are in the right order. They are then cut to size and bound together to make a book.

Reading with your fingers

a	b	c
d	e	f

Books for blind people are printed with raised dots, called the Braille alphabet. The dots stand for different letters which readers can feel with their fingertips and make out the words.

Art

People often disagree about art. One person may say a painting or a sculpture is beautiful but another person may think it is very ugly.

A work of art can be made in many different ways. Each of these artists is working on a different type of art, using different materials.

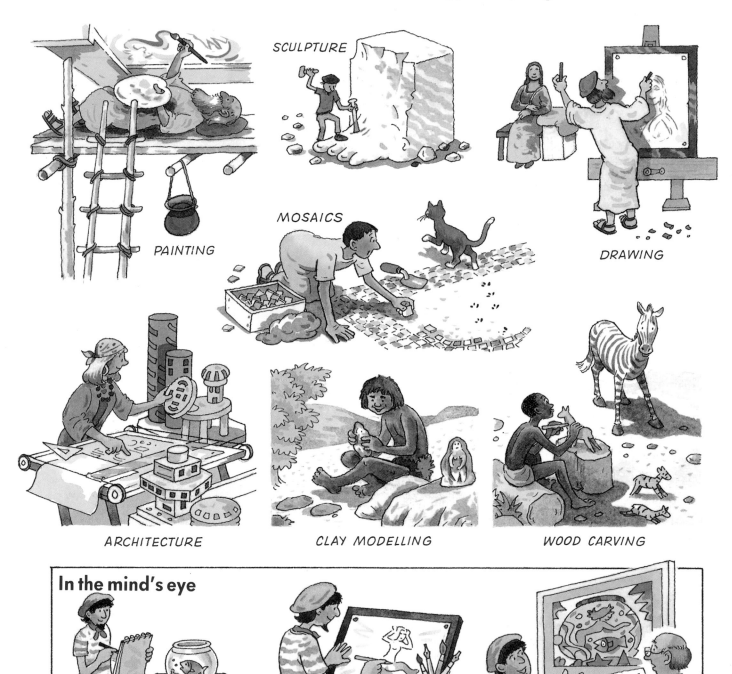

PAINTING

SCULPTURE

DRAWING

MOSAICS

ARCHITECTURE

CLAY MODELLING

WOOD CARVING

In the mind's eye

Artists may work from real life and copy what they see.

Some artists may use only what they see in their mind.

Many artists mix real life and their imagination to create a work of art.

Art changes with the times

Different styles of art go in and out of fashion as people's tastes change. Until about 500 years ago most of the pictures painted by European artists were of religious scenes.

Some art, such as Chinese painting, is traditional. This means that artists have all worked in the same way for hundreds of years without changing their style.

People may be so used to certain styles of art that they are shocked or amused when an artist tries something new.

New types of art are often the result of new inventions. When the camera was invented people took up photography as an art form.

Fame, fortune and forgery

Some artists worked all their lives but no one bought their paintings and they were very poor. They became famous after they had died.

In the past, wealthy people, called patrons, paid an artist to work because they believed the artist had talent.

Works of art by famous people and ancient works of art are often very valuable. They sell at auctions for very high prices.

Clever forgers can imitate famous artists' work so well that people are fooled. They pay a lot of money for something that is a fake.

Music

What is music?

Music is lots of sounds put together to make a tune.

Not everyone likes the same sort of music.

How sounds are made

There are three main types of musical instrument which are played in different ways.

Instruments which you play by blowing are called wind instruments.

Instruments which you play by tapping or banging are called percussion instruments.

Instruments which you play by plucking or stroking strings are called string instruments.

The oldest music

People made music by singing or chanting long before they invented musical instruments.

A person who sings alone is called a soloist. Two people singing together is a duet.

A choir is a group of people who sing together or sing different parts of the same song.

Why play music?

Music helps people work. Galley slaves on ships used to row in time to drum beats.

People play music to celebrate special occasions such as birthdays and weddings.

Usually people play music to entertain themselves and their friends.

Passing music on

Traditional music, called folk music, is often so old that no one can remember who first wrote it. Some folk music, such as Scottish reels, have become popular around the world.

In the Middle Ages, people invented a way of writing down music. People who write music are called composers. They may write music for one instrument, for many instruments, or songs.

The orchestra

An orchestra is a large group of musicians who play traditional instruments. The musicians watch a conductor, who signals them to join in and keeps them playing together.

Bands

BRASS BAND

JAZZ BAND

STEEL BAND

Bands are small groups of players who may play only one sort of music on their instruments.

Some bands have instruments which they can play as they walk around. Others stay in one place.

Crafts

What are crafts?

All through the ages people have hand made things to use in their everyday lives. They often decorate what they have made so that they look colourful and attractive.

People around the world are skilled at different crafts. All these craftspeople are at work on their speciality.

ENGLISH BASKET MAKING

MEXICAN WEAVING

TURKISH CARPET MAKING

PUEBLO POTTERY FROM NEW MEXICO

SPANISH LACE MAKING

GREEK WOOL SPINNING

AFRICAN GOLD JEWELLERY

MOROCCAN CLOTH DYEING

VENETIAN GLASS BLOWING

Mastering a craft

In the Middle Ages, boys called apprentices worked in their master's workshop for seven years, learning a craft.

Craftsmen were proud of their work and employed 'searchers' to stop shoddy work from leaving the workshop.

A master craftsman was someone who had finished his apprenticeship and was an expert at his trade.

Crafts for sale

For thousands of years people have taken their craftwork to open-air markets to sell.

Sometimes they exchange their work for things they need but do not know how to make.

In the past travelling traders and merchants went from country to country.

They bought wares from craftsmen in one place and then sold them somewhere else.

Endangered crafts

Things made by hand are never exactly the same. Many craft-workers sign their work.

In the past, craftworkers often knew their customers and could make things to suit them.

Later on, people invented machines which could make lots of identical things.

The machines were much faster and cheaper than craftspeople so many old crafts died out.

Making up for lost time

Fine examples of some crafts are now valuable.

This is because a lot of craftwork was made for everyday use, and so was thrown away if it broke.

Some people are interested in learning old crafts so that they become popular again and do not die out.

They often sell their work as souvenirs to tourists.

Dressing up

Why do people wear clothes?

People wear clothes that suit the work they do. Fishermen wear waterproof clothes and boots that will not slip.

In some jobs people wear uniforms so they can be recognised if people need them

Clothes for climates

People wear clothes to suit the weather. In hot, damp places they wear very little and so keep cool.

On special ceremonial occasions important people wear clothes that show their power, authority and position.

Sports clothes are light and easy to move in. Players may wear the same colours to show they belong to a team.

In hot, dry climates people wear long robes which shield them from the Sun's rays.

Some people like to wear clothes that attract attention and make them stand out in a crowd.

Some people who want to show they all belong to a special group wear the same sort of clothes or uniform.

In cold climates people wear layers of clothing. The warm air trapped between the layers keeps out the cold.

Keeping up with fashion

The way people dress changes with the times they live in. Four hundred years ago men wore high heels and stockings.

Clothes that were once very popular often seem ridiculous to people who live now.

Clothes that once shocked people by their daring, soon became commonly accepted and worn.

Old and new clothes

A country's traditional dress, such as the Indian sari, is called their national costume.

Most modern clothes are made by machines. They are easy to wash, cheap and comfortable.

Some people pay a fortune to have clothes specially made for them by a famous fashion designer.

Other ways of dressing up

All over the world, hair has always been an important part of dressing up. Masai men in

Africa spend days doing each other's hair. The women shave their hair as a sign of beauty.

At one time in Europe, fashionable people hid their own hair under elaborate wigs.

Since prehistoric times people have worn make-up. Nowadays it is used to attract attention to lips and eyes.

Some people, such as the Nuban men from Sudan, paint their bodies all over to make them look strong and healthy.

Tattoos are a sort of permanent make-up. The pattern is pricked into the skin and colour added.

People dress up with jewellery. In Laos, women wear the family savings to show their wealth.

Some people wear jewellery to show they are married. Indian women wear nose rings.

Sometimes the jewellery a person wears shows that they belong to one religion. Christians may wear a cross.

Myths

Long ago people made up stories to explain mysteries and things that they did not understand, such as thunder and lightning. These stories are called myths.

Many of the Ancient Greek myths were about their gods. They thought the gods often appeared on Earth as real people. Zeus, king of the gods, made thunder to frighten his enemies.

How did the world begin?

A North American myth

In this myth, a raven created the world. He dropped pebbles into the ocean to make land. Then he created the trees and grass, fish, birds and animals. Finally he made men and women out of pieces of clay and wood.

A Nigerian myth

In this myth, Mother Woyengi sat on a special stone and made people out of handfuls of earth.

She put the people who chose lives of luxury into a fast, dangerous stream, the rest into a slow, clear stream.

A Norse myth

In this old Norse myth, the centre of the universe was a huge tree called Ash Yggdrasil.

For nine nights, Odin, the one-eyed god, hung upside down from the tree to learn poetry, the secret of magic.

King Arthur and the knights of the round table

The Celtic myths about King Arthur told throughout medieval Europe and ever since, are based on a real king who once ruled in Britain.

Arthur had 1,600 good and brave knights. They fought many great battles against invading enemies, rescued people and killed monsters.

Can myths change history?

The Aztecs of South America told stories about Queztalcoatl, a fair-skinned god, who would come to Earth in a certain year.

That very year a Spanish explorer, named Cortes, sailed to South America looking for a new land to conquer.

The Aztecs thought Cortes was Queztalcoatl because he was fair-skinned and came in a ship, so he easily beat them.

Dragons

Stories about dragons have been told all over the world for centuries. Hawaii, China, Wales and Iceland all have places named after them.

Dragons lived in water and frightened people by breathing fire. Heroes in myths often have to kill a dragon to save everyone's life.

Heroes

Many myths tell the adventures of a hero who is searching for something special, such as the secret of life.

Creatures great and small

In an Ancient Greek myth, a giant called Atlas held the world on his shoulders to stop it from falling out of the sky.

Tiny spirit people are called fairies. Leprechauns are Irish fairies who must give gold to anyone who can catch them.

Modern myths

Myths can be about the future as well as the past. Today, many films are about heroes travelling through time and space to new worlds.

Stories about the future are called science fiction. Like ancient myths they are based on people's latest theories about the universe.

Religions

People who follow a particular religion believe in a spiritual world and share the same ideas about life and death.

There are many religions around the world. Each one has different beliefs, customs and rules for how its followers should behave.

Judaism

Jewish people believe that a man called Abraham first told people to believe in one God. He was a 'Prophet'.

They believe that God chose them to keep his laws which are written in the first part of the Bible.

Christianity

Christians believe God sent his son, Jesus, to teach people how to live. His story is in the second part of the Bible.

Christians say Jesus taught them to love one another, to pray and to teach other people about God. They worship in a church.

Islam

A prophet called Muhammad, from Mecca, taught his followers, Muslims, to pray five times a day to their god, Allah.

Their religion is called 'Islam' which means to obey Allah by praying, fasting (not eating for a while) and helping the poor.

Hinduism

Hindus believe that after you die, you are born again, either as an animal or as another person. If you have been good

during your first life, your next life will be a better one. At Hindu festivals, dancers dress up as gods, such as

Ganesh the elephant-god. Most Hindus believe their gods are really all one god, called Brahman, in disguise.

Buddhism

A man called Buddha began Buddhism among Hindus in India. Later, Buddhism spread to Asia, China and Japan. In Bangkok, Thailand, there is a line of 394 golden statues of Buddha.

Buddhists believe you should give up luxuries and live a simple, peaceful life. They say that you live more than once, but that eventually you can escape to a place of spiritual peace.

Religions without gods

Some eastern religions, like Taoism, have no gods. Taoists say everything in life is sacred because it is part of nature.

They believe all things are either female (called Yin) or male (called Yang). Yin and Yang balance each other.

Taoists want people to live simply and fit in with nature. They should try to be like a stick floating in a stream.

Rituals

Nearly every small community or tribe in the world has a religion, with its own rituals, songs and dances.

What do witch doctors do?

Some American Indians believe that sickness and bad luck are caused by evil spirits who work through witches and sorcerers.

People who have had bad luck ask their witch doctors to drive the evil spirits from their homes, using beads, feathers and pipes.

Where do dead people go?

Some people believe that you go to another world as an invisible spirit when you die.

People put flowers on graves to show they have not forgotten the person who has died.

Others, who think spirits stay on Earth disguised as animals or people, leave gifts for them.

Theatre and dance

Why do people dance?

Dancing probably began as a way for people to celebrate something or to worship gods.

People also danced to tell a story, to make their crops grow or to bring luck in a fight.

Ballroom dancing began at court as a way for ladies to show off their beautiful dresses.

Nowadays, people dance to keep fit, meet others, follow the latest fashion and for fun.

People laughed at dances such as the tango and the twist, until they became popular.

Inventing dances

Choreographers are people who make up the movements and steps dancers perform.

Ways of dancing

There are many ways of dancing. You can dance alone or with a partner, you can follow set steps or make it up yourself. Modern dance is freer and less formal than traditional dance.

Indian dancers move their hands, eyes and bodies more than their feet. Whirling dervishes stomp and twirl in rhythm. Russian dancers crouch down and kick out their feet very fast.

What is ballet?

A simple form of ballet began two hundred years ago at the Italian and French royal courts.

Classical ballet is a difficult dance done on the toes which takes years of training to learn.

The Russians made ballet more exciting by making the music and dance tell a story.

Where did theatre begin?

People have always acted out stories, but the Ancient Greeks built the first theatres. People could go and watch plays.

Actors wore frowning masks if they were in a tragedy (a sad play), and smiling masks if they were in a comedy (a happy one).

Travelling players

In the Dark Ages there were no theatres in Europe. Acrobats, minstrels and jugglers travelled around entertaining people.

Behind the scenes at the theatre

Powerful lights shine on the main actors as they speak. Someone controls the lights from the side of the stage.

Actors often dress up in costumes to look like the person they are supposed to be in the play.

A director tells the actors how to act their parts in the play, when to move and how to say their speeches.

Scenery and props (objects used in the play) are often put on the stage to make it look more realistic.

The person who writes the play is called a dramatist.

Opera

Opera began in Italy. In an opera the actors sing their lines to music instead of speaking them. Operas usually have an orchestra, colourful costumes and scenery.

What is mime?

Mime means acting without words. The mime artist shows his feelings by making faces and moving his body. In Japan whole plays, called Kabuki, are acted in mime.

Education

What is education?

Some teachers think that children are like pots, waiting to be filled with information.

Others think teaching should be like lighting a fire – one question leads to many ideas.

Education can mean finding out how to do things and learning how they were done before.

Why learn things?

People learn things for many different reasons but they all help them to live better lives.

YOU CAN WRITE THINGS DOWN IF YOU WANT TO REMEMBER THEM OR SHARE THEM WITH OTHERS.

LEARNING A FOREIGN LANGUAGE HELPS YOU TO UNDERSTAND SOMEONE FROM ANOTHER COUNTRY.

Quel horreur!

It's your fault!

MOST PEOPLE AROUND THE WORLD LEARN THE THINGS THEY NEED TO SURVIVE, SUCH AS HOW TO GROW FOOD AND BUILD THEIR HOMES.

FINDING OUT ABOUT NUMBERS AND LEARNING HOW THINGS WORK HELPS PEOPLE TO COPE WITH MACHINES AND LOOK AFTER THEIR MONEY.

NOWADAYS MANY PEOPLE HAVE MORE FREE TIME TO LEARN SPORTS AND HOBBIES AND OTHER WAYS OF HAVING FUN TOGETHER.

When do you learn?

The minute you are born, you start learning by copying people around you. You learn a lot before you are five.

When you go to school, you are taught the basic things you need to know. Trying something out is a good way of learning.

No matter how old you are, you can learn something new. Someone who knows a lot about a subject is called a specialist.

Education in other times and places

Many years ago boys in Sparta, in Ancient Greece, were trained to be fit and brave so that they could fight their enemies.

In the past girls were taught different things from boys, such as sewing and cooking. This is still true in some places today.

Two hundred years ago there were few schools. Children who had rich parents were taught at home by a tutor.

There were no free schools until many people began to live and work in big cities. Governments paid for schools out of taxes.

Not everyone has a choice about what to learn. Mexicans in Patzcuaro have to learn how to make hats for a living.

These Bolivian children are having fun at school learning a traditional dance. One day their own children may learn it.

Education today

Half the children in the world are now taught in schools which they go to for several years.

As well as ordinary schools, there are many kinds of special schools.

People of all ages can go to these schools to learn all kinds of different subjects.

When they leave school, some people go to a college to learn more about a subject.

Inventions such as television and computers have made new ways of learning possible.

Lessons beamed round the world by satellite can be shared by people in different places.

Government and politics

What is a government?

If people lived together without any rules, they would disagree about how things should be done and get in a muddle.

To avoid this, they choose some people to organize things and make laws. This is called the government.

What is politics?

Politics is about people deciding how to live together. The ones who think the same way form political parties.

Leaders

A dictator is a leader who decides how to run the country without asking what people want. He does not let his people vote. Some kings and emperors were dictators.

If a leader refuses to listen to what people want, they sometimes get angry and take over the government of the country by force. This is called a revolution.

Why do people vote?

Most countries hold an election every few years. Most of the adults can vote for the people they want to run things.

The country is split up into areas and you vote for someone from your area. Those who win most votes form the government.

People who want to be in the government try to win votes by promising to run the country in a better way.

Can you change things?

People who get together to try to change something are called a pressure group. They pressurize the government to make new laws. If there are enough of them, this often works.

Until 1918 women in Britain were not allowed to vote. Many joined a pressure group called the suffragettes. They held demonstrations and tied themselves to railings to get what they wanted.

What governments do

The government looks after many different parts of everyday life.

People pay money called 'taxes' to provide all these things:

Most governments run the airlines, railways and transport systems which people use to travel around.

One part of the government looks after education in schools and colleges. It pays for research in art and science.

A part of the government provides a police force and courts to keep law and order.

Some governments take care of people's health by paying for hospitals and doctors.

When countries trade with each other the government helps things to run smoothly.

Most countries keep armed forces and weapons in case there is a war.

Some governments build parks, museums, and places for people to enjoy themselves.

Air and water

What is air?

The Earth is wrapped in a layer of air, called the atmosphere. Air is made of several different gases. One of them is oxygen which people and animals need to breathe to stay alive.

Air is all around you, but you cannot see it. You can feel it, but only when the wind is blowing against you. The wind is moving air.

Air spreads

Air does not have any special shape. It spreads out in all directions and is everywhere.

Air pushes

If you go on blowing air into a balloon, it will burst, because the air pushes so hard against the inside of the balloon.

When a parachute falls, it traps air underneath it. The air pushes up against the parachute, making it fall slowly.

Hot air rises

When air is heated, it expands and takes up more space. The hot air is lighter than the cold air around it and rises upwards.

Hot air balloons lift off the ground because hot air inside them makes them lighter than the air around them.

A gas burner heats the air inside the balloon. When it is switched off, the air inside it cools and the balloon lands.

Trapped air

Trapped air keeps things warm. Wool clothes feel warm because wool has many fibres which trap a lot of air.

Birds fluff up their feathers in winter to trap air under their feathers to keep them warm.

Air presses

Air presses against you, but your body is made so that you do not feel the weight.

What is water?

Water is liquid. It has no shape of its own, but takes the shape of whatever is holding it.

If water is poured into a glass it will fill the glass, and become the same shape as the inside of the glass.

If water is spilt on the floor, it runs all over the place, because it has nothing to keep it in a particular shape.

Where does water go?

A puddle of water will dry up on a sunny day. The water does not really disappear. It turns into tiny drops, too small for you to see.

The drops, called water vapour, rise into the air. When water turns into water vapour and rises into the air, it is called evaporation.

The air is full of water vapour, because heat from the Sun makes water evaporate from the seas, lakes and rivers.

As water vapour rises it reaches cold air high in the sky. It turns back into tiny drops of water which join to make clouds.

The drops fall to the ground as rain. Water vapour turning into water again is called condensation.

Water pushes

If you stand in a swimming pool with water up to your neck and your arms by your sides, your arms will slowly rise. The water pushes them up.

Why does an iron ship float?

An iron ship floats because it pushes aside so much water. The more water something pushes aside, the harder water pushes up against it.

Light and colour

Nearly all our light comes from the Sun. Light from the Sun gives us days and nights. As the Earth spins around the Sun, the side facing the Sun has daylight, while the other side is dark.

Light travels in straight lines. It cannot go around things. So there are dark shadows behind things that stand in its way.

Things that light can pass through, like glass, are called transparent. Things it cannot pass through, like people, are called opaque.

Splitting light

In 1666, Isaac Newton shone a beam of sunlight through a piece of glass called a prism.

The light that came out of it was broken up into all the colours of the rainbow.

Newton had discovered that ordinary white light is made of many colours mixed together.

What makes a rainbow?

When sunlight shines through rain, we sometimes see a rainbow, because each drop of water behaves like a tiny prism.

The raindrops break light into its different colours, making a rainbow. Rainbow colours are always in the same order.*

From the ground, a rainbow looks like an arch. From an aeroplane, it looks like a circle.

*You may not always see all the colours in a rainbow.

Bouncing light

Light bounces off surfaces just like a ball bounces off things. This is called reflection.

If you shine a torch on a mirror, you can see light bounce. All light you see is reflected.

The sunlight that enters our atmosphere is reflected by millions of tiny bits of dust and droplets of water.

In a cinema you see the beam of light between the projector and screen because dust in the air reflects the light.

Black Space

Outer Space is totally dark because there is no dust or water to reflect light.

The moon does not give out any light of its own. You can only see it because it reflects the light of the Sun.

Why do we see colours?

We see colours because things absorb or reflect varying amounts of light.

When light shines on snow, all the light is reflected back, so the snow looks white.

When light shines on soot, all the light is absorbed, so the soot looks black.

A red flower looks red because it reflects the red part of light, and absorbs the rest.

A green car reflects the green part of light and absorbs the rest, so it looks green.

Seeing red?

Most animals cannot see colour. A bull charges at a red flag because it is waved not because it is red.

103

Electricity

Electricity that stays

There are two sorts of electricity. One is called static electricity. It stays in the same place. You can sometimes hear it crackle when you take off nylon clothes.

Electricity that moves

The other sort of electricity is called current electricity. It flows through things. This sort of electricity is used to light and heat our houses, and is used to run machinery.

Discovering electricity

The Greeks knew, 2,500 years ago, that rubbing amber with fur made sparks of static electricity. Scientists did not learn how to make current electricity until about 150 years ago.

Electric machines

Michael Faraday invented the first electric motor in 1821. Machines run by electric motors are now used in many houses and in factories, where they do the work of many people.

Conductors

Some things, like metals, allow electricity to flow through them. They are called conductors. Metal wires are used to conduct electricity from one place to another.

Insulators

Things electricity cannot flow through, like plastic and rubber, are called insulators. Wires that carry electricity are covered in plastic to protect people from electric shocks.

How does a battery work?

A battery makes electricity with special chemicals. When all the chemicals are used up, the battery stops working.

Electricity from batteries is not as powerful as electricity from plugs. But batteries can be taken and used anywhere.

Danger!

ELECTRICITY CAN GIVE YOU A DANGEROUS ELECTRIC SHOCK. NEVER PLAY WITH PLUGS OR WALL SOCKETS OR ANYTHING THAT IS PLUGGED IN.

Where does our electricity come from?

The electricity in our houses, streets and factories comes from big power stations that make it in large quantities.

The power stations make electricity with fast running water from rivers, or by using the heat from burning coal or oil, or from nuclear power.

ELECTRICITY PYLON

POWER STATION

THICK WIRE CABLE

ELECTRICITY WIRE

UNDERGROUND CABLE

SWITCHING ON A LIGHT LETS ELECTRICITY FLOW IN THE WIRES.

Electricity flows from power stations along thick wire cables. The cables are carried high above the ground by pylons to towns.

In towns, the cables run underground to each house. The electricity is then carried around the house through wires built into the walls.

What's in a plug?

Plugs have metal prongs which allow electricity to flow through them. When a plug is put into a socket and switched on, electricity flows through the prongs and along the wires.

Why does a light bulb make light?

Electricity flows through a coil of special metal in a light bulb. The metal becomes so hot that it glows white, giving out light. The first light bulb was made in 1879 by Thomas Edison.

Lightning is electric

During thunderstorms, static electricity may jump between a cloud and the ground. It makes a powerful flash of light, called lightning, and can damage or set fire to anything it strikes.

Lightning always takes the shortest route to the ground, so it is dangerous to shelter under a tree during a storm. Tall buildings have metal conductors to carry lightning safely to earth.

Sound

What is sound?

When air vibrates or moves very quickly backwards and forwards it makes a sound. When you speak, or even whisper, cords at the back of your throat, called vocal cords, vibrate.

The vibrations push the air, so that the air vibrates too. These invisible vibrations, called sound waves, spread out through the air, like the ripples when you drop a stone in a pond.

How do you hear?

There are things in your ears, called ear-drums, which work like drums. They vibrate when sound waves hit them.

The speed of sound

Sound waves travel at about 340 metres per second. When an aircraft flies faster than sound, you hear a bang.

Thunderstorms

In a storm you see lightning before you hear the thunder it makes because light travels faster than sound.

Silent space

RADIO WAVES CAN TRAVEL THROUGH SPACE.

Sound waves need air to travel through. If there was no air you would not hear anything at all.

On the moon, where there is no air, astronauts have to talk to each other by radio.

Echo! Echo!

HELLO HELLO HELLO HELLO HELLO HELLO

Sound waves sometimes bounce off surfaces, such as the underneath of bridges. When this happens you hear an echo.

High and low sounds

The faster something vibrates, the higher the sound it makes. The vibration made by a mosquito beating its wings up and down very fast makes a very high sound.

A bee beats its wings more slowly than a mosquito, making a lower sound. The highness or lowness of sound is called its pitch and the number of vibrations a second is its frequency.

Animal hearing

Many animals can hear sounds that are too high pitched for people to hear.

Dogs can also hear sounds from much further away than people. Farmers use special whistles to send them signals from far away.

Telephone

The telephone was invented in 1875 by Alexander Bell. There are now nearly 500 million telephones in the world.

On the telephone, the vibrations made by your voice are turned into electric signals by a microphone.

Wires carry these signals over long distances, so you can telephone people far away. Wires even run under the sea.

The person you call hears your voice because a loudspeaker in their telephone turns the signals back into sound.

Radio waves

Radio waves are all around you, but you cannot hear them. They travel very fast, at the speed of light.

Radio stations turn sound waves from voices or music into radio waves. These waves travel through the air to radios.

Radios turn radio waves back into sound waves you can hear. You can listen to many programmes on the radio.

Ships use radios to contact each other or the shore. Aircraft crews use radios to speak to the control tower.

Television pictures

Television pictures are filmed by special cameras that turn pictures into electric signals.

A television set picks up radio waves and turns them back into sound and pictures.

Transport by land

Making tracks

Until about 5,000 years ago there were no roads and people could only go as fast as they could run, so they did not go far. The first roads followed animal tracks, like the bush trails people cut through the forests in Africa.

Dragging loads

To build the pyramids, the Ancient Egyptians needed blocks of stone that were too heavy to drag over the ground. They moved the stones by putting them on wooden sleds and pulling them along on rollers made of tree trunks.

Riding

About 4,000 years ago, people began to tame horses. A person could travel ten times faster on horseback than on foot.

Harnessing

At about the same time the harness was invented. Now people could use strong animals to pull heavy loads.

On the road

Travelling was easier on good roads. The Romans built thousands of kilometres of straight, paved roads.

The wheel revolution

The first wheels were probably made about 5,000 years ago by the Sumerian people. They built carts and fixed solid wooden wheels to them, to carry food to trade with other villages.

The Ancient Greeks used chariots on wheels to go to war. They put spokes in the wheels to make the chariots lighter and faster and added wooden rims so that the wheels lasted longer.

Carriages and coaches

About 250 years ago rich people in Europe rode in horse-drawn carriages. Roads were bumpy, so travel was uncomfortable.

Stage coaches were the first kind of public transport. Every 20 km or so they stopped at an inn to change the team of horses.

Crossing America in a wagon

The pioneers of the nineteenth century travelled vast distances across North America and South Africa in covered wagons.

A team of oxen or horses pulled them. Inside there was room for a family and enough food and water to last for weeks of travel.

The age of the train

In 1825 the first steam train to carry passengers ran on a railway line from Darlington to Stockton, in Britain, at 24 kph.

People could travel further and faster by train. By the 1930s a train called *Hiawatha* was able to cross the USA at 160 kph.

Most modern trains run on diesel fuel or electricity. In Japan the world's busiest railway carries 112,000 people daily.

How the car started

Two German engineers, Benz and Daimler, built the first petrol-driven car in the 1880s.

Early cars had wooden, spoked wheels, oil lamps, and no roof. They often broke down.

In 1889 John Dunlop invented air-filled rubber tyres to give a smoother ride.

At first, cars were built by hand and were very expensive. Between 1908 and 1928, Henry Ford produced 20 million cheaper cars in a factory in the USA, so many more people could buy them.

Cars with powerful engines and bodies shaped to cut through the wind can travel very fast. In 1983 a car called *Thrust 2*, with a jet engine, went at over 1,000 kph in Nevada, USA.

Ships

Setting sail

The Egyptians built the first ships out of reeds 5,000 years ago, to cross the River Nile.

They had a papyrus sail which helped them move when the wind was behind them.

When they wanted to sail into the wind, the slaves had to paddle the ship along.

Round ships

For thousands of years, Arab traders have built small ships, called dhows, to carry cargo. They have triangular sails which can be turned to catch the wind and sail in any direction.

Long ships

The Vikings in Scandinavia were the first to cross the Atlantic to North America in about AD 900. Their long, sturdy ships had a big square sail and were steered by a large oar.

Voyages of discovery

By 1500, ships in Northern Europe had grown very big, with up to four masts and many sails. In these ships, explorers discovered routes across the Atlantic and to India and China.

SAILORS CLIMBED THE MASTS TO LET OUT OR TAKE IN THE SAILS.

THE SHIPS WERE STEERED WITH A RUDDER.

A sailor's life was hard and dangerous. He slept in a dark, crowded cabin and lived on salted meat, dry biscuits and water.

Clippers

In the 1800s, huge, sleek cargo ships, called clippers, raced to carry tea from China to Britain and wool from Australia to the USA.

With their tall masts and many sails, they could travel up to 640 km in 24 hours, in a strong wind, and could cross the Atlantic in 14 days.

Steam ships

In 1838 the first wooden ships to be driven by steam engines crossed the Atlantic.

Steam turned paddle wheels on each side and they had sails in case they ran out of coal.

Propellers

In the 1850s, iron ships driven by a screw propeller were built. They did not depend on the wind so they could run to timetables.

Luxury liners

During the 1930s huge steel ships called liners were built to carry passengers between Europe and North America in great comfort and luxury.

Oil tankers

One of the largest ships ever built is the oil tanker, *Globtik London*. It is 379 m long, so the crew use bicycles to get around on deck.

Nuclear submarines

In 1960 a US nuclear-powered submarine went around the world, underwater, in only 83 days at depths of 300 metres.

Hovercraft

A hovercraft can travel over flat land or water. It skims along on a cushion of air made by powerful fans.

Hydrofoils

Hydrofoils are the fastest type of watercraft. They have underwater wings to lift and speed them above the water.

Flying machines

Taking off

For hundreds of years people tried to fly by copying birds. They built wings from feathers and jumped from high places.

They always crashed because human chest muscles cannot flap wings fast enough to keep a human body in the air.

Balloons

Since 1783 people have flown in baskets lifted by balloons filled with hot air, but they only go the way the wind blows.

Gliding down

In 1891 a German named Otto Lilienthal ran down a hill strapped to a hang-glider he had built. The air trapped under the wings lifted him off the ground and he glided gently down.

The Wright flyer

The Wright brothers made the first powered aeroplane flight of 36.5 metres in 1903. They built their own petrol engine to drive two propellers fixed to a glider frame.

Record breakers

Early aeroplanes were light and unstable, and the engines often failed. Flying them was exciting but dangerous.

In 1909 Louis Bleriot made the first powered flight across the Channel from France to England in only 37 minutes.

Amy Johnson flew from England to Australia in 1930. It took 19 days because she had to stop to refuel her plane.

Passenger flights

By the 1930s, aircraft with four engines were able to carry up to 30 passengers as fast as 193 kph. Flying became a fast and comfortable way to travel a long distance.

Modern jumbo jet aircraft can carry hundreds of passengers at speeds of up to 969 kph. Flying has become so popular that every minute an aircraft lands somewhere in the world.

Supersonic speed

Aircraft that go faster than the speed of sound are called supersonic. When they reach that speed they make a loud bang.

The first supersonic jet to carry passengers is *Concorde*. It travels at 2,333 kph, and can fly from New York to London in three hours.

Helicopters

A helicopter has a propeller on its roof to lift it straight upwards, so it can take off from any piece of ground.

Helicopters cannot fly faster than 300 kph, but they fly up and down as well as along, and they can hover in one place.

They are useful for dropping cargo or rescuing people from the sea or on mountains where aircraft cannot land.

Rocketing into space

Rockets travel faster than any other craft. They shoot into the air pushed by hot gases made by burning liquid fuel.

Space shuttles

Space shuttles take off like rockets but they have wings so they land like aircraft.

By the 1960s the Americans and Russians had built huge rockets powerful enough to carry people into Outer Space.

In 1969 a rocket called *Apollo 11* flew 384,400 km to the moon in three days, and a man landed there for the first time.

Rockets can only be used once, but space shuttles can carry scientists on many trips to Outer Space.

Medicine

What is medicine?

Medicine is not just what you take when you are ill. It also means how to cure people and stop them getting ill.

What is illness?

Most illness is caused by germs getting into the body. Germs are tiny living things, so small that you cannot see them.

Your body reacts to these germs by showing signs, which doctors call symptoms, such as a rash or temperature.

Seeing the doctor

When you are ill, the doctor finds out what is wrong by studying your symptoms. Each illness has its own symptoms.

The doctor may say you need a medicine. There are thousands of medicines and the doctor has to choose the right one for you.

Danger!

ALL MEDICINES CAN BE DANGEROUS. NEVER PLAY WITH THEM AND NEVER TAKE ANY MEDICINE WITHOUT ASKING A GROWN-UP FIRST.

Medicines

Antibiotics are medicines that work by killing the germs in your blood which make you ill. The first one, penicillin, was discovered in 1928.

Some medicines, called analgesics, can make you feel better by making the pain go away or by bringing your temperature down, but they do not kill the germs. Aspirin is an analgesic.

Other cures

Some people have other ways of curing illness. Acupuncturists push fine needles into the skin, without hurting the patient.

Homeopathic doctors use tiny amounts of medicines made from plants and minerals to treat illnesses.

First Aid

First Aid is the first thing you do to help someone if they have an accident. Knowing what to do may save their life.

Preventing illness

Preventing people from becoming ill is as important as curing illness. Looking after your body by eating healthy food and taking exercise makes you healthier and can prevent illness.

Vaccines

Doctors give vaccines to stop you catching some diseases. A vaccine is a small dose of germs in your blood that makes your body fight a disease.

Hospitals

People go to hospital for tests and special treatments. Sometimes they need an operation. Most mothers also have their babies in hospital.

MEDICAL SCIENTISTS STUDY SAMPLES TAKEN FROM PATIENTS, SUCH AS BLOOD.

NURSES DO A LOT OF DIFFERENT JOBS LOOKING AFTER PATIENTS. MIDWIVES HELP MOTHERS TO HAVE THEIR BABIES.

SPECIALLY TRAINED DOCTORS CALLED SURGEONS DO OPERATIONS IN A ROOM CALLED THE OPERATING THEATRE.

EVERYONE WEARS SPECIALLY CLEANED CLOTHES, RUBBER GLOVES AND MASKS TO STOP GERMS SPREADING.

PATIENTS ARE GIVEN AN INJECTION TO MAKE THEM SLEEP DEEPLY SO THAT THEY DO NOT FEEL ANY PAIN.

X- RAY PICTURES OF YOUR INSIDES ARE TAKEN TO SEE IF ANY BONES ARE BROKEN.

SPECIALISTS ARE EXPERTS ON ONE PART OF THE BODY, SUCH AS BONES.

Blood Bank

Blood is stored in a Blood Bank. It is given to anyone who has lost a lot of their blood in an accident.

What makes things go?

Things do not move by themselves. Something must push or pull them.

The Earth pulls

You have to push a ball into the air by throwing or kicking it. The ball comes back to the ground because of gravity.

Gravity is the pull of the Earth which attracts everything to it. You cannot see gravity but you can see what it does.

Gravity makes leaves fall to the ground and rivers run downhill. If there was no gravity, things would spin off the Earth.

Muscle power

Thousands of years ago, people only had their own muscles to do all their work.

Then they learned to use animals, such as oxen and donkeys to pull ploughs and to carry heavy loads.

They learned to make simple machines, such as levers and pulleys. These made their work easier and faster.

They could use them to lift and build things which were much too heavy to be moved by muscle power alone.

Power from nature

People learned to use moving water and wind to work machines.

The Egyptians used the wind to push their boats along, 5,000 years ago.

The first water-wheels were built about 2,000 years ago along rivers where the current of water turned them.

17TH. CENTURY WATER-WHEEL, SYRIA

They were used to bring water to the fields and to turn millstones that ground grain.

For more than a thousand years, until steam engines came into use, water-wheels were the main source of power for making many machines work.

GREEK WINDMILL

DUTCH WINDMILL

Windmills depend on wind so they could be built in high places where there were no rivers or streams. The first windmill in Europe dates back to 1150.

Power from steam

The first engine to be invented was the steam engine, about 200 years ago. Steam engines were powerful and could do greater tasks than any of the earlier machines.

They could run huge machines in factories. Early steam engines burnt coal or wood to make them work. *

Since the first steam train was built in 1803, for about 100 years, almost all trains were driven by steam engines.

AMERICAN STEAM TRAIN

BRITISH STEAM TRAIN

*You can read more about steam engines on pages 68 and 69.

Carriages were invented that were powered by steam engines. They moved very slowly.

Boats driven by steam engines were built a hundred years ago. They were the first boats that could travel without needing the wind or water currents.

Power from inside

A new type of engine, called the internal combustion engine, was invented in 1860. Instead of burning fuel outside the engine like a steam engine, it burns fuel inside the engine. This means it can be smaller than a steam engine.

Petrol engines in cars, diesel engines and jet engines are all internal combustion engines.

The first power-driven and controlled flight was made in 1903 by an aeroplane with a petrol engine.

Today, diesel-electric locomotives run high speed passenger trains.

Most passenger aeroplanes today have jet engines. Jet engines have turbines, which are many-bladed wheels that spin very fast.

Many ships today are driven by turbines.

Turbines can be made to spin by burning fuel or by flowing water. Water turbines in dams make a quarter of the world's electricity. This is called hydro-electric power.

Electricity is carried by cables and wires to homes and factories. There it is used to work many different types of machines.*

Rocket engines

Rocket engines work in the same way as jet engines except that rockets carry their own supply of oxygen. They do this because fuel cannot burn without oxygen and there is none in Space.

Making machines go

The fuel for internal combustion engines must be able to flow into the engine to be burnt. It must be liquid, so coal and wood are of no use.

The internal combustion engine was only workable once fuels, such as gas and oil, were discovered in the last century.

Coal and oil are called fossil fuels because they are made from the remains of plants and animals that lived hundreds of millions of years ago.

Today, so much oil is used that there is a danger that the supply will run out.

So people are looking for new ways of making electricity, such as using heat from the Sun or power from the wind.

WINDMILL   SOLAR PANEL

Nuclear power

Nuclear power stations make electricity. The first nuclear power station was built in 1954 in the USSR and others have now been built in many countries.

*You can read more about electricity on pages 104 and 105.

Machines and inventions

Over the last 100 years many machines and gadgets have been invented to make homes more comfortable and easier to keep clean.

Vacuum cleaners

Vacuum cleaners were invented in 1904. Bellows, worked by hand, sucked up dust.

The first vacuum cleaners to work by electric motor were sold in the USA from 1908.

Washing machines

People began to use simple washing machines in the 1900s. Clothes were put into a wooden tub and tumbled by turning a handle.

By 1920 washing machines were fitted with motors, but the clothes still had to be fed by hand through a mangle to wring the water out.

Modern washing machines can be programmed to soak, wash, spin and dry the clothes on their own.

Irons

In the 1850s ironing was a slow task. Irons were heated by blocks of metal warmed in the fire.

By 1890 electrically heated irons had been invented. The latest irons press clothes by dampening them with jets of steam.

Baths and showers

Until the 1850s baths had to be filled and emptied by hand so they were usually small and shallow.

One type of bath, built in 1900, had a shower fixed to it. Someone pumped water out of the bath to spray the bather.

By 1900 some baths had cold water piped to the taps. The water was heated by a gas boiler under the bath.

Today most houses have bathrooms, supplied with hot water piped from a central boiler.

Toilets

Toilets that flushed waste into the sewers when a chain was pulled were invented in 1888.

Today toilets are quieter but still work in much the same way.

Cookers

Until the 1800s most cooking was done on open fires. Then iron ranges burning coal or wood were invented.

In the 1860s gas cookers were invented that could be turned on and off to give heat instantly.

In the 1930s cookers were fitted with thermostats to hold the oven temperature steady.

At the end of the 1950s a new, much faster way of cooking food by microwaves rather than by heat was invented.

Refrigerators

For hundreds of years people have stored food by packing it in ice. In 1890 home refrigerators were invented to keep food cool and fresh.

Between 1912 and 1915 Clarence Birdseye began to freeze food to keep it fresh for longer. Many households now freeze their own food.

Central heating

The first central heating systems, in Ancient Rome, heated the whole house with warm air from a furnace underground.

In the mid 1800s coal- and wood-fired boilers which warmed radiators were invented.

Some new houses have hot-air vents built into the walls of every room. The air is heated by gas or electricity.

Air conditioning

Air conditioning was introduced in the USA in 1911 to keep people's homes cool.

Clocks

Grandfather pendulum clocks were first made around 1670 in London. They keep accurate time to within 2 minutes a day.

In 1929 quartz chips were used in clocks to make them accurate to within one second in 3 years.

Pins and zips

Safety pins were first made in the USA in 1849. Before that, people used brooches to pin clothes.

A new, quick way of fastening clothes together – the zip – was invented in 1913 by a Swedish engineer.

Sewing machines

Around 1856 people began to use sewing machines worked by hand or foot treadle to make clothes at home.

The latest sewing machines are electronic. They can sew many different stitches at the touch of a button.

Lenses

In 1609 Galileo used spectacle lenses to build an early telescope. He used it to see stars that had not been seen before.

Microscopes were invented in Holland in 1590. They magnified tiny things, such as bacteria, through strong lenses.

Cameras

Cameras were invented in 1839. Early cameras took photographs on coated paper or glass, which was very slow.

In 1889 the first portable Kodak cameras were invented. They used a new kind of flexible roll film which meant they could take photos more quickly and cheaply.

Modern cameras are extremely accurate. They can even take photos in the dark.

Typewriters

Typewriters were invented in the 1870s. Until this century most people in offices wrote everything by hand.

With the latest electronic typewriters some people can type 90 words in a minute.

Record players

Wind-up clockwork record players called gramophones were invented in the 1880s. At first the records were hard to hear.

Modern electric hifi systems produce a much clearer sound and play music in stereo out of two speakers.

At first inventors tried to make records out of wax, tinfoil and even chocolate. Today they are made from plastic.

Radios

The first radios were made in the 1920s. They only made a faint sound so people had to listen to them on headphones.

In the 1950s portable radios became possible because transistors were invented. One small transistor can replace many parts radios need.

Televisions

Television began in the 1930s. Early sets had a tiny screen showing flickering black-and-white pictures.

By the 1960s television was being broadcast in colour. Nowadays people with video recorders can record TV programmes or use video cameras to make their own films.*

*Find out more about new technology on page 120.

New technology

This century, discoveries in electronics have led to a revolution in technology which has changed the way we live.

Information

In the past, information was stored on paper in the form of books, newspapers or timetables.

People needed huge filing systems and libraries to store information.

Then, at the beginning of the century, people began to experiment with electronics (ways of controlling electricity).

Scientists invented valves which could control the flow of small currents of electricity.

These valves were used as amplifiers and made the first radios possible.

They were also used to make the first computers in the 1940s.

These huge machines filled a whole room. They could do calculations but not much else.

The silicon chip

In 1958 the silicon chip was invented. A chip is a tiny little slice of silicon only a few millimetres square.

ENLARGED SILICON CHIP

It contains hundreds of electric circuits and can control almost any machine, as long as they have been programmed to work together.

Lots of machines you use everyday, such as washing machines, televisions, cameras and telephones work automatically as they are controlled by chips.

Computers

The invention of the chip meant that people could make smaller, faster, computers that could do more than ever before.

Modern computers can do calculations very fast, move information about and store it.

A computer can look up the electronic equivalent of a library of books in a split second, to tell you if a book is there.

Airline computers are linked to others all round the world and can tell you at once which tickets are available for which flights.

Videotex makes it possible for you to call up information from a computer so that it appears on your television screen.

It gives you access to thousands of pages of useful information.

Robots

Robots are automatic machines which are controlled by computers.

They can be programmed to do different jobs, but cannot think or do anything on their own.

Most robots cannot move but stay in one spot. They are like big arms with a gripper at the end.

They are mainly used in factories to do work that is repetitive or dangerous. They are very strong and tough.

They are also useful for doing jobs in Space in conditions which would be difficult for people.

The space shuttle can be fitted with a long folding robot arm. It uses this to launch satellites and other machines or to repair them when necessary.

New materials

Plastics have revolutionized life both at home and work.

The first plastic was made in 1869 from plant cellulose. It was hard but it could be shaped when heated.

During the 1930s new types of plastic were made from chemicals found in coal.

In 1935 nylon was made from chemicals. It was a cheap copy of silk and was used to make underwear and stockings.

Polyesters were invented in the 1940s. From the 1950s onwards many plastics were made from petroleum-based chemicals.

Modern plastics you use everyday include vinyl, silicone polish, adhesives, cling film and plastic bags.

Space exploration

New technology has made the exploration of Space possible.

Satellites are unmanned spacecraft launched by rockets which orbit the Earth. The first, Sputnik 1, was launched in 1957 from the USSR.

TELSTAR (USA) SATELLITE

There are about 300 satellites in orbit today. They are used to send telephone calls and television pictures around the world and for weather information.

Astronauts have orbited the Earth, have walked in Space and have landed on the moon.

VIKING 1 (USA) ON MARS

Unmanned spacecraft have been sent to explore distant planets. They have sent back information and pictures, and have even landed on Mars and Venus. Voyager 1 (USA) flew by Saturn in 1980, Uranus in 1986, and is expected to reach Neptune in 1989.

Lasers

Lasers are machines which make light. The first was made in 1960.

TORCH LIGHT

LASER LIGHT

Unlike ordinary light, which spreads out and is made of many colours, light from a laser goes in one direction only and is made of one colour. *

It makes the brightest light known, even brighter than the Sun.

Light from a laser is so strong and makes so much heat that it can be used to cut, drill and weld strong metals.

LASER BEAM

STEEL

DRILL

Surgeons use lasers to operate on patients. As well as making a fine cut, the heat from the laser seals up the wound.

Lasers can make holograms. These are three dimensional photographs: they look like a solid object hanging in the air in front of you. When you look at a hologram from a different angle, you get a different view of the picture.

Laser beams can make recordings and play music and video discs.

VIDEO DISC PLAYER

Lasers are used to measure distances by counting how long it takes for the light to reach something.

EARTH

LASER BEAM

MOON

In 1962, a laser was pointed at the moon to calculate its distance from Earth. Scientists saw the light reflected on the moon just over two seconds later.

*You can read more about light and colour on pages 102 and 103.

Index